D0371335

John Millington Synge was born in 1871 of an old Anglo-Irish family. Due to ill-health he was educated mainly by private tutors before studying at Trinity College Dublin and the Royal Irish Academy of Music. He went to Germany to continue his musical studies in 1893 and then, turning to literature, moved to Paris in 1895. There he met W. B. Yeats, who suggested he go to the Aran Islands to live with the islanders as one of themselves and to 'express a life that has never found expression'. He spent a few weeks on the islands each year from 1898 to 1902. *The Aran Islands* did not appear until 1907, but it was his experiences in Aran that gave him the plots of his plays *In the Shadow of the Glen* (1903), *Riders to the Sea* (1904) and *The Well of the Saints* (1905). His emergence as a playwright coincided with and furthered the Irish dramatic revival. He was first a literary adviser and then a director of the Abbey Theatre in Dublin, where the first performances of his plays provoked violent controversies. His most famous work, *The Playboy of the Western World*, which was suggested by an anecdote he had heard in Aran, unleashed a riot in the theatre at its first performance in 1907. Synge was in love with the young actress, Molly Allgood, who played the principal female role in this play, and it was she who inspired his play *Deirdre of the Sorrows*, left unfinished at his early death in 1909. Another of his earlier plays, *The Tinker's Wedding*, had been regarded both by Synge and Yeats as too dangerous to put on in Dublin, and it was not seen there until 1971.

Tim Robinson was born in England in 1935, studied mathematics at Cambridge and taught the subject in Turkey. He then worked as a visual artist under the name of Timothy Drever, first in Vienna and later in London, where there were several exhibitions of his abstract paintings and environmental installations in the

1960s. In 1972 he went to live in the Aran Islands, and began writing and making maps. He now lives in Roundstone, Connemara, where he and his wife run the Folding Landscapes studio, which publishes his maps and related writings on the west of Ireland. His two volume study of the Aran Isles, *Stones of Aran: Pilgrimage* and *Stones of Aran: Labyrinth*, is available in Penguin.

J. M. SYNGE

———

THE ARAN ISLANDS

EDITED WITH AN INTRODUCTION
BY TIM ROBINSON

PENGUIN BOOKS

PENGUIN BOOKS

Published by the Penguin Group
Penguin Books Ltd, 80 Strand, London WC2R 0RL, England
Penguin Putnam Inc., 375 Hudson Street, New York, New York 10014, USA
Penguin Books Australia Ltd, 250 Camberwell Road, Camberwell, Victoria 3124, Australia
Penguin Books Canada Ltd, 10 Alcorn Avenue, Toronto, Ontario, Canada M4V 3B2
Penguin Books India (P) Ltd, 11 Community Centre, Panchsheel Park, New Delhi – 110 017, India
Penguin Books (NZ) Ltd, Cnr Rosedale and Airborne Roads, Albany, Auckland, New Zealand
Penguin Books (South Africa) (Pty) Ltd, 24 Sturdee Avenue, Rosebank 2196, South Africa

Penguin Books Ltd, Registered Offices: 80 Strand, London WC2R 0RL, England

www.penguin.com

First published 1907
Published in Penguin Twentieth-Century Classics 1992

17

Introduction Essay and Notes copyright © Tim Robinson, 1992
All rights reserved

The moral right of the author has been asserted
The acknowledgements on p. li constitute an extension of this copyright page
Filmset in 10/12 pt Monophoto Imprint

Printed in England by Clays Ltd, St Ives plc

Except in the United States of America, this book is sold subject
to the condition that it shall not, by way of trade or otherwise, be lent,
re-sold, hired out, or otherwise circulated without the publisher's
prior consent in any form of binding or cover other than that in
which it is published and without a similar condition including this
condition being imposed on the subsequent purchaser

Contents

PLACE/PERSON/BOOK

Synge's *The Aran Islands*

It begins: 'I am in Aranmor, sitting over a turf fire, listening to a murmur of Gaelic that is rising from a little public-house under my room', and it ends: 'The next day I left with the steamer.' It does not mention why he came, nor what bearing the island of time represented between these two sentences was to have on his further life. Its exclusion of matters relating to the past and the future of the Aran Islands, except as they arose in thought and conversation during his visits, is equally absolute. This self-sufficiency of the book commands respect, and to present some additional information on its subject and on its author, before discussing it in detail, is not to buttress it, but to erect a base on which to display its singularity.

THE PLACE

The word *ára*, literally the kidneys or loins and, by extension, the back, is a common element of Irish place-names, in which it connotes a back or ridge of land, and so Oileáin Árann, anglicized as the Aran Islands, could be translated as 'the ridge islands'.* The three islands, when they come into view against the Atlantic horizon as the ferry leaves the shelter of Galway

---

*The largest of the three islands is called Árainn (the obsolete locative case of *ára*) or Árainn Mhór (*mór* 'big'); the latter name was anglicized as Aranmore or Arranmore. Nowadays the name Aranmore is reserved for the island off Co. Donegal. Perhaps it was to avoid confusion with the Donegal island that the Ordnance Survey in 1839 introduced the name Inishmore for the big island, in line with the anglicized forms of the neighbouring islands' names, Inishmaan and Inisheer, and despite the fact that there was then no Irish form Inis Mór ('big island') to be anglicized. Sadly the dull backformation Inis Mór is now widely used even by native Irish speakers, and the euphonious Árainn is

Bay, are clearly the remains of a long escarpment broken through by the ocean. They once formed part of the Burren uplands to the south-east in Co. Clare, from which they are divided now by five miles of water. The sounds between the islands are each about a mile and a half wide, and ten or twelve miles separate Árainn from Connemara to the north. Aran (the island group as a whole can be so named, for brevity) is of limestone, like its parent the Burren, and the formations to which limestone gives rise determine much of the character of the Aran landscape and even many features of daily life there. Stone is what meets the eye everywhere. Along its north-east-facing flank the escarpment rises in a few broad terraces separated by low cliffs or scarps, and the treads of these giant steps are level expanses mainly of bare rock, riven by long parallel fissures and littered with broken fragments and boulders in some areas, as smooth as a dance-floor in others. Inis Meáin (Synge uses the anglicized form, Inishmaan) has the most spectacular examples of this extraordinary limestone 'pavement', as it is called, spreading like a succession of grey aprons below the villages. In each of the islands, settlement is largely in the lee of the upper scarps, while from the sheltering ridge above the string of villages, uninhabited expanses of rough stony pasturage decline very slightly south-westwards, and in Árainn (Synge's Aranmor) terminate with dramatic suddenness in vertical or deeply undercut cliffs fifty to three hundred feet high opposing the Atlantic. All the lower shores of the islands except for a few sheltered stretches facing north-east carry a 'stormbeach' of shingle or boulders heaped by the waves into a rampart above the high-water mark, which even continues along the tops of the lower stretches of cliff. Again Inis

---

neglected. Inis Meáin, anglicized as Inishmaan, means simply 'middle island'. The name of the third and smallest island has been rather corrupted; anciently it was Inis Oirthir, 'island of the east', and the form now recommended by the Ordnance Survey, Inis Oírr, anglicized as Inisheer, is an attempt to represent the current pronunciation while remembering the old meaning. Synge often refers to it as the south island, and to Árainn as the north island – the island chain runs from east-south-east to west-north-west.

Meáin has the most breathtaking example of this formation. Around its exposed south-western tip thousands of blocks up to the size of cars and cottages have been broken by the sea out of the low rock-terrace forming the shoreline, shifted hundreds of yards inland and assembled into a vast dyke; and where the coastline rises into cliffs along the west of the island the stormbeach follows it, diminishing as it gradually rises out of range of all except the most exceptional waves and fading out at a height of about a hundred feet (at which point the last few stones of it have been at some unknown period formed into a little clifftop look-out shelter, now called Synge's Seat).

Aboriginal soil is rare in Aran; the glaciers of the last Ice Age scoured the rock bare, and most of what soil developed after that has long been lost to erosion. It is likely that the islands were wooded, perhaps until settlement and grazing increased in early medieval times, but for centuries there have been virtually no trees apart from low thickets of hazel on sheltered slopes. The little green fields on the northern sheltered flank of the islands are the work of generations of men, women and children who cleared the crag of loose stone and spread it with sand and seaweed carried up in baskets from the shore. The field boundaries are dry-stone walls, of which there are about a thousand miles in the three islands, so that most of the terrain is a mosaic of fractions of acres. This apparently manic multiplication of walls has its purposes, in shielding stock and crops from the high winds of the oceanic coast, in facilitating the close control of grazing – so that the cow has to eat up all the grass, not just the juicier sorts, before it is allowed into fresh pasture – and in freeing the ground from the litter of stone. Again, Inis Meáin, the stoniest of the three stony islands, has the tallest walls – well over head-height in places, making an oppressive and bewildering maze of the rough tracks that ramify and dwindle like veins throughout the tissue of little rectangular fields.

But Aran's porous limestone is a kindly rock, unlike the impermeable granite of the opposite coast of Connemara, where the soil is acidic and waterlogged and brings forth rushes and, over millennia, great depths of bog. Aran has no bog, and until a few decades ago many south Connemara shore-dwellers lived by cutting turf from their bogs and shipping it to the Aran Islands as fuel. Aran's limy soil, stony and shallow though it is, crops well; her cattle were prized and her potatoes paid the Connemara boatmen for their turf. Nowadays farming on the tiny scale permitted by Aran's craggy terrain is not a paying proposition, and the hazel scrub is invading abandoned fields. The small usage of pesticides and fertilizers means that the paradoxically exuberant flora of such limestone karstland is still present in its plenty. Aran's drifts of common buttercups and daisies are such as cannot be seen now in the rundown countrysides of Europe, while her harsh geology and mild oceanic climate provide habitats for unusual floristic neighbourings; thus arctic-alpine flowers like the Spring Gentian bloom in patches of shallow soil on the exposed surfaces of the pavement, close to such Mediterranean species as the Maidenhair Fern flourishing in the damp shelter of the rock-clefts. It is the Atlantic that dispenses this climate, shipping in constant weather changes from the south-west: interleaved squalls and shafts of sunshine that dress the islands in rainbow after rainbow, halcyon calms that curdle into sea-mist, storms that blow themselves out like candles.

The islands' spider-webs of field-walls entangle many archaeologies tumbled one upon another: communal tombs like big boxes of limestone slabs from the late Stone Age, stone-lined cist graves from the Bronze Age, huge dry-stone cashels of the Celtic Iron Age, primitive oratories and hermits' cells, foundations of once famous monasteries, roofless medieval chapels. The cliff-edge cashel of Dún Aonghasa, with its three semicircular ramparts, the inner one thirteen feet thick and eighteen high, abutting on to empty space nearly three hundred feet above the surge of the Atlantic, occupies the most dramatic site of Celtic Europe. This, together with six other great cashels, of which Dún Chonchúir on the central height of Inis Meáin is the most impressive, shows that Aran was for some centuries around the beginning of our era the seat of a settled and prosperous community, for there is no evidence to justify the traditional designation of these mysterious structures as 'forts'. It has been suggested that the cashels were primarily ritual centres;* if so, the religious significance of Aran had been long established when St Enda came here some time before AD 489 (according to the much later medieval account of his life and miraculous works) and founded a monastery which was to become known throughout Europe. Columcille of Iona, Ciarán of Clonmacnois and Colman of Kilmacduach were among the saints to whom hagiography ascribes the almost obligatory early years of prayer and study in the illustrious and uniquely blessed isles called 'Aran of the Saints'. According to a poem by the ninth-century king-bishop of Cashel, Cormac mac Cuillenáin, it is impossible to count the saints of Aran, the four holiest places in the world are the Garden of Paradise, Rome, Aran and Jerusalem, no angel ever came to Ireland without visiting Aran, and if people understood how greatly the Lord loves Aran they would all come to partake of its blessings. It was not until the decade of Synge's first visits that Aran briefly recovered something of this extraordinary mystic status.

Throughout the early centuries of the growth of the Normans' walled town of Galway, the Aran Islands belonged to the O'Briens, the traditional Irish rulers of Munster. In the 1560s it was captured from them by the O'Flahertys, a former ruling family of Connacht who had long been confined to the wildernesses of Connemara by the Norman advance. In trying to regain their lost islands the O'Briens appealed to the new system of law emanating from England, and Queen Elizabeth took the opportunity of appropriating the islands, which in the context of her war with Spain were of some strategic importance, and granting them to an Englishman on condition he maintain a garrison there. A fort was built in Árainn, which had its days of drama in 1652, when Parliamentarian soldiers

---

*Etienne Rynne, 'Dún Angus: Fortress or Temple?' in *An Aran Reader*, eds. Breandán and Ruairí Ó hEithir (Dublin, 1991).

were crushing the last gasps out of the Irish rebellion which had broken out in response to England's Civil War. Aran had surrendered to Cromwell's general when he took Galway city, and then was recaptured by an expedition from the Confederate Catholics' last strongholds in Connemara and Inishbofin. The Parliamentarians shipped 1,300 footsoldiers and a battering-piece out to Aran and, having finally secured the castle, proceeded to enlarge it with ancient stone from the ruined churches and the round tower of St Enda's monastery. For a time Aran was a holding camp for half-starved Catholic priests rounded up by the fanatically Protestant regime of the Commonwealth. There was an English military presence on Aran thereafter until early in the next century, with the result that today Aran's bloodgroup pattern is similar to that of northern England, where Gaelic and Saxon stock have intermingled.*

Aran's population, like that of Ireland as a whole, was at its peak just before the Great Famine of 1845–9, but the islands seem to have ridden the demographic storm more smoothly than Connemara, for instance, where many villages were totally abandoned. In 1841 there were 3,521 persons in the three islands; in 1851 there were 3,333. The potato-blight seems to have been less severe in Aran than on the mainland, and it is said that only one person on the islands died of starvation in those years. But the leech of emigration had been applied to the Aran community, which has never since been able to shake it off. By Synge's time the population was 2,863 (421 of them in Inis Meáin), and today it is about 1,350. The fragmentation of the terrain into tiny fields expresses the desperation of those nineteenth-century generations, hoarding every tuft of grass for their cattle. Inordinate rents drained the community of capital, forced it to live almost exclusively on potatoes and made its life an unceasing struggle, in the stony fields, in little wooden boats and canvas currachs on the sea, or collecting seaweed and

*E. Hacket and M. E. Folan, 'The ABO and RH Blood Groups of the Aran Islanders', *Irish Journal of Medical Science*, June 1958.

burning it for kelp* on the shore. As in much of rural Ireland, long-suffering exploded into violence against the exploiters in the 1880s.

The very seclusion of Aran had occasionally attracted revolutionary influences before that date. It is said that after the defeat of the French invasion of 1798 and the rebellion that welcomed it in Mayo, there was a French officer on the run here with numerous United Irishmen, one of whom set up a hedge-school in Árainn. Similarly some of the hunted leaders of another revolutionary generation, Young Ireland, passed through after their pitiful attempt at a rising in 1848; John Blake Dillon was sheltered for a time by the people of Inis Meáin and, according to a locally conserved account, was secretly visited there by his colleague William Smith O'Brien. Later on the Fenian conspiracy had members among the Aran tenantry, so that when the Land League came into existence in 1879 it found in Aran as elsewhere a nucleus of political awareness and even a number of activists armed with guns stolen from the local police barracks.

Aran was at this time the property of absentee landlords, the Digbys of Landenstown in Kildare.† Its owners knew little of such a remote source of a tiny fraction of their rents as the Aran Islands, which were administered for them by agents

---

* For the kelp industry, see note 20 on p. 142.

† The Rev. Simon Digby, Protestant archbishop of Elphin, had acquired half of Aran in 1713, and Robert Digby bought out the other half in 1744. At the time of the Great Famine of 1847 the landowner, Miss Elizabeth Francis Digby of Landenstown, Kildare, was criticized for sending only two tons of meal as relief to her hungry tenants. According to local lore, Miss Digby visited the islands once, when a dance was held in her honour on a stretch of smooth limestone near Cill Mhuirbhigh; there was a spot known as Miss Digby's Steps by the harbour in Cill Éinne, but otherwise little was known of her by the islanders. A niece of hers had married Sir Thomas St Lawrence, Third Earl of Howth, in 1851, and when Miss Digby died in about 1894 the two daughters of that marriage, Henrietta Eliza Guinness (sister-in-law of Lord Ardilaun) and Geraldine Digby St Lawrence, inherited. The islands were acquired from the St Lawrences and the Guinnesses by the Land Commission in 1922.

who themselves visited only periodically. The more immediate power over the islanders' lives was the O'Flaherty family of Kilmurvey House in Árainn, a dwindled branch of the Connemara O'Flahertys; they had built up a holding of the best of the land, from which other tenants had been evicted for non-payment of rent, and sublet much of it to the less fortunate. Patrick O'Flaherty* and his son James, each in his turn chief middleman, Justice of the Peace and representative of civility in the islands, were in a position of almost feudal power, and they bore the brunt of the islanders' accumulated resentments when Aran, like much of the rest of rural Ireland, was shaken by the Land War. In 1881 the Land Leaguers drove the O'Flahertys' cattle over the highest cliffs of Árainn, a deed still remembered but only reluctantly spoken about in the islands. Aran life at that time was further embittered by involved disputes, boycotts and scandals arising out of attempts by the little Protestant elite – the Church of Ireland minister Mr Kilbride, the landlord's agent, an evangelical school-teacher and others – to persuade the lower orders of the sinfulness of papistry. This murky series of events was copiously reported in the Galway press and in such national organs as the *Freeman's Journal*; Aran was well known to be one of the most hard-done-by communities in all the immiserated West. A branch of the National League was founded in the islands in 1886 to organize support for Home Rule, and rapidly became a power in the community. When the government responded to the terrorism of the Land War not only by coercion but by reform, and tried to 'kill Home Rule by kindness', Aran shared in the benefits. In 1885 a Land Court sitting in the islands' capital, Cill Rónáin (anglicized as Kilronan), reduced rents by forty per cent.† The Aran fishing industry had dwindled almost to extinction in the dreadful years of recurrent hunger since the 1840s. In 1891 the Congested Districts

---

* See note 27 on p. 144.

† Oliver J. Burke, a barrister who visited Aran for this purpose, wrote the first book on the islands, *The South Isles of Aran* (London, 1887).

Board* was set up by the government to develop those localities of the West in which the population far exceeded what their productive capacities could support. A steamer service from Galway had already been established in that year, and on this basis of access to markets the Board undertook to nucleate a modern fishing industry, by paying a bounty to boats from Arklow to come and work out of Aran, by inaugurating a telegraph link to the mainland and by improving the harbours.

While thus badgered and solicited by sectarian and secular politics, the Aran Islanders also found themselves elected to a literary and even a metaphysical status by the romantic nationalism which was transforming Ireland's image of itself. Successive generations of Irish thinkers – many of them members of the Protestant Ascendancy – were founding their separatist claims on the rediscovery of the Celtic soul, essentially at odds with the mundane progressivism of the Anglo-Saxon. And this ancient, mysterious, spirit guide of the nation was to be called forth from the humble cottages of the last living representatives of Celtic purity, the Irish-speaking farm- and fisherfolk, and pre-eminently those of the western seaboard. Aran, that forlorn outcrop of want, was to become one of the chief shrines of this Ireland of the mind.

The rediscovery of Aran's Celtic and monastic magnificence had been begun by George Petrie, 'the father of Irish archaeology',† in 1821; it was consolidated by the excited reports of John O'Donovan in 1839 when he was employed by the Ordnance Survey to record Ireland's ancient monuments, and crowned in 1857 by the visit of the Ethnological Section of the British Association, who, accompanied by many Irish scholars and led by Dr William Wilde,‡ feasted within the walls of Dún Aonghasa. The enlistment of the contemporary islander in the reconstruction of Irishness followed closely. Here all that was most pungently characteristic of this relict state of being had been hoarded, like treasure buried in troubled times, now to be

---

* For the Congested Districts Board, see note 1 on p. 137.

† For Petrie, see note 2 on p. 137.

‡ For Wilde, see note 2 on p. 137.

disinterred. Petrie had also collected folksongs, and O'Donovan place-names, from the Irish-speaking natives; the poet Samuel Ferguson and the painter Frederick Burton made the life of the Aran fisherfolk their subjects. The living culture of Aran, it was realized, was a repository of venerable antiquities. The Celticist Kuno Meyer visited Inis Meáin. Foreign scholars – the linguists Pedersen of Copenhagen and Finck of Marburg, the medievalist Zimmer of Berlin, the folklorist Jeremia Curtin* of America – made the pilgrimage and paid their respects in learned treatises. The islands' ancient monuments were re-examined by an excursion of the Royal Society of Antiquaries of Ireland in 1895, and in the same year the Irish Field Club Union, with the naturalist Robert Lloyd Praeger, came to marvel at their fauna and flora. The revival of the Irish language, in retreat for centuries, was the dream of such founder members of the Gaelic League as Eoin MacNeill and Fr Eugene O'Growney,† who sought out the living language in Aran in the 1880s. W. B. Yeats came in 1896, looking for a setting for his proposed novel, *The Speckled Bird*, which was to oscillate between mystical Paris and peasant Ireland. In the year of Synge's first visit, 1898, the young Patrick Pearse was there and founded an Aran branch of the Gaelic League, and Lady Augusta Gregory collected fairylore. Thomas Mac-Donagh, later to be Pearse's colleague at his school, St Enda's in Dublin, and to join him in the sacrificial Easter Rising of 1916, also spent time in Inis Meáin, where he organized rifle

---

* For Pedersen, Finck and Curtin, see note 2 on p. 138. Kuno Meyer (1858–1919) studied at Leipzig; while lecturing on German and Celtic at Liverpool 1884–1906, he travelled widely in Scotland, Wales and Ireland and founded the School of Irish Studies in Dublin in 1903. He succeeded Zimmer in the chair of Celtic philology at Berlin in 1911. Heinrich Zimmer (1851–1910) was in Aran in 1880 and supported the Land Leaguers at a public meeting; he published a paper on St Enda in 1889.

† For the Gaelic League, Douglas Hyde, MacNeill and Pearse, see note 30 on p. 144. Fr Eugene O'Growney (1863–99) first visited Inis Meáin in 1885 as a student at the Catholic seminary of Maynooth; he became Professor of Irish at Maynooth in 1891 and began to publish his famous *Simple Lessons in Irish* in 1893.

practice on the crags. Thus by Synge's time Aran, and Inis Meáin in particular, had been widely identified as the uncorrupted heart of Ireland. (This attribution of a particular degree of Gaelic purity to the middle island was first made by Petrie, who thought that the morals of the big island had been contaminated by people introduced to build the lighthouse in 1818, and those of Inis Oírr by its proximity to the Clare coast.) The cottage of Páidín and Máire MacDonncha, in which Synge stayed, became known as Ollscoil na Gaeilge (the University of Irish) from the number of scholars who lodged there, and it was very reasonable of the islanders to conclude, as one of them told Synge, that 'there are few rich men now in the world who are not studying the Gaelic'.

Nowadays each of the islands has its airstrip, its small industries and its electricity generators. But the increasing implication of Aran with the outside world since Synge's day has scarcely dulled its alluring legend. The American director Robert Flaherty's famous 1932 'documentary', *Man of Aran*, situated his hero in a timeless world of rock and wave, and the many subsequent treatments in words and images have threatened to bury the little islands Pompeii-deep in interpretations. If Ireland is intriguing as being an island off the west of Europe, then Aran, as an island off the west of Ireland, is still more so; it is Ireland raised to the power of two. Whether the grain of wonderful truth in this can survive the trampling of the hundred thousand tourists who now visit the islands each year, remains to be seen.

THE PERSON

The Synges came to Ireland in the seventeenth century from England, produced a succession of bishops for the Protestant Church of Ireland, and married land. J. M. Synge's father, John Hatch Synge, was a younger brother of the owner of Glanmore Castle in Co. Wicklow; he inherited a small estate in Co. Galway, became a barrister in Dublin, and married the daughter of an Ulster-born rector of intemperate evangelical zeal. As landowners and clerics of the established church, standing on the apparently natural and divinely sanctioned economic and cultural rights of the Anglo-Irish community in Ireland, families like the Synges were loftily remote from such aboriginals as the Catholic, Irish-speaking and illiterate peasantry of the Aran Islands. At the same time the ties between the two classes were close and necessary (at least to the well-being of the former). The Synges' income derived in part from the rents paid by the small tenants of their Galway estates (as J. M. Synge's mother sharply reminded him once, when his social conscience was troublesome), while for his proselytizing forebears the rural Irish were a field of souls for the harvesting; in fact Synge's uncle had been the Church of Ireland minister in the Aran Islands in the 1850s.

But by J. M. Synge's generation the attitudes of the Anglo-Irish to the peasantry had become more complex and problematic, as the Protestant hegemony cracked before the rise of the Catholic middle classes. Among the Synges' peers were some of the intellectual leaders of the new version of Irish nationalism which found its inspiration in the hitherto despised folk of the countryside – but the Synge family itself had no truck with such an abdication of the duties of civilization.

John Millington Synge* was born in 1871 in Rathfarnham, then a village, now absorbed into the suburbs of south Dublin. His father died in the following year, and Mrs Synge, left with five children and a reduced income, moved to a house next door to her mother in nearby Rathgar. John was a sickly asthmatic child, and laboured under the burden of his mother's vivid belief in hell-fire. An early love of the countryside and wildlife afforded some relief from the fond oppressions of home, but his reading of Darwin (when he was fourteen) introduced the new pain of religious doubt. Within a few years he no longer regarded himself as a Christian, but as a worshipper of a new goddess, Ireland. His disbeliefs and beliefs formed

---

* The factual framework of the following is drawn from the standard biography, David H. Greene and Edward M. Stephens, *J. M. Synge 1871–1909* (revised edition, New York and London, 1989).

rift-valleys of incomprehension between himself and his relatives, though he always preserved his status as a member of the
family household. He gulped the patriotic balladry published
in a nationalist newspaper, the *Nation*, and scoured the
countryside in search of the Irish antiquities he read about in
the writings of George Petrie. And in Petrie he would have
read:

> The Araners are remarkable for fine intellect and deep sensi-
> bility ... If the inhabitants of the Aran Islands could be con-
> sidered as a fair specimen of the ancient and present wild Irish
> ... those whom chance has led to their hospitable shores to
> admire their simple virtues, would be likely to regret that the
> blessings of civilization had ever been extended to any portion
> of the inhabitants of this very wretched country. But, fortu-
> nately for them, they cannot be so designated; much of their
> superiority must be attributed to their remote, insular situation,
> which has hitherto precluded an acquaintance with the vices of
> the distant region.*

Synge's enthusiasm for Irish matters did not close his mind
to a wider cultural heritage. He took up the violin, and, while
scraping through a second-class degree at Trinity College,
which introduced him to the Irish language† and to Hebrew,
he worked for and won a scholarship in counterpoint from the
Royal Irish Academy of Music. It seemed that music was
going to be his life. In 1893 a distant relative, Mary Synge, a
concert pianist, arranged for him to stay with friends of hers,
the Von Eiken sisters, in Oberwerth on the Rhine. After two
months of studying music there, he moved to Würzburg. But
he came to feel he would never be sufficiently confident to
perform in public, and that his compositional talents were of
little worth. He moved to Paris, and in 1895 he commenced
courses in modern French literature, medieval literature and

*Quoted in Dr William Stokes, *Life and Labours in Art and Archaeology of George Petrie* (London, 1885).

† Synge's substantial attainments in the knowledge of the Irish language and
its literature, together with his changing attitudes to the policies of the Gaelic
League, are discussed in detail in Declan Kiberd, *Synge and the Irish Language*
(London, 1979).

comparative phonetics at the Sorbonne, with the idea of becoming a critic of French literature. He lived the student's life of
cold attics and introspective scribbling; he read such subtle
adversaries of his mother's simple words of God as Mallarmé,
Huysmans and Baudelaire. Holidays with his family in Wicklow alternated with a visit to Rome and further eclectic studies
in Paris: the anarchist Sébastian Faure, Marx, Morris, Pet-
rarch, St Thomas à Kempis's *The Imitation of Christ* (whose
discipline of meditative practice he seems to have tried to
adapt to aesthetic contemplation). In Ireland he was pursuing
an unpromising attachment to a girl called Cherrie Matheson,
the daughter of a Unionist barrister prominent among the
Plymouth Brethren; she would not have him because of his
atheism. On the Continent he got to know a number of young
women with whom he corresponded – all too often, some of
them felt, on the subject of Cherrie – and with whom he
obviously found it easier to form close friendships than with
the men of his aquaintance.

In 1896 W. B. Yeats, who was a member of the secret Irish
Republican Brotherhood, and his even more revolutionary
muse Maud Gonne were in Paris, founding L'Association Irlan-
daise ('the Irish League') as a focus for Irish nationalists in
France. Synge met Yeats in December of that year and joined
the League, but soon resigned: 'I wish to work in my own way
for the cause of Ireland and I shall never be able to do so if I
get mixed up with a revolutionary and semi-military movement.' But other sides of the multifaceted Yeats probably influenced him, through such works as *The Celtic Twilight*, which
enlists the fairies and ghosts of the Irish countryside into the
shadowy battalions of European mysticism. Like so many
others at that period he 'dabbled', as they say, in psychical
research, in company with a new friend, Stephen MacKenna.
MacKenna, then an impecunious journalist, had already translated *The Imitation of Christ* and was soon to begin his life's
great work, the translation of the Neo-Platonist philosopher
Plotinus.* But whatever degree of objective existence Synge

*George Steiner (*After Babel*, New York and London, 1975) writes, 'Mac-

might have allowed to the manifestations of the seances, he was always too much the realist to have shared Yeats's prodigal credences as expressed in *The Celtic Twilight*: 'Everything exists, everything is true, and the earth is only a little dust under our feet.'

It was probably at a meeting of the League that Yeats (according to his own account written in 1905) issued his momentous command: 'Give up Paris, you will never create anything by reading Racine, and Arthur Symons will always be a better critic of French literature. Go to the Arran Islands. Live there as if you were one of the people themselves; express a life that has never found expression.' Yeats had recently visited Aran with Symons, and, as the strategist of the Irish cultural revival, he realized the islands' symbolic importance, but knew that the new recruit would be better equipped than himself for their re-taking.

But before Synge could go to Aran, he had an appointment with the disease that was to kill him twelve years later. The lump on his neck for which he went under the knife in December of 1897 was recognized by his doctor and the hospital nurses as a symptom of Hodgkin's disease, a cancer of the lymphocytes; it seemed they did not reveal this to him, and it was eight years before the growth recurred, but in the light of some very specific imaginings of death in his notebooks of the Aran years, it is difficult to believe he did not suspect the truth.

Synge returned to Paris for the first three months of 1898 and, perhaps with the Aran Islands in mind, interested himself in France's own Celtic appendix. He read Le Braz's *Vieilles Histoires du Pays Breton*, and Pierre Loti's *Pêcheur d'Islande*, about Breton fishermen who spend the summer seasons fishing off Iceland. It appears from a draft of his introduction to *The Aran Islands* that Synge intended to form his work on the

---

Kenna gave his uncertain physical and mental health to the translation of Plotinus' *Enniades*. The five tall volumes appeared between 1917 and 1930. This solitary, prodigious, grimly unremunerative labour constitutes one of the masterpieces of modern English prose and formal sensibility.'

model of Loti's. How that could have been done is an intriguing question, since Loti's novel is the story of a doomed romance, in which the sea as bride asserts its primacy over the seafarer's village love. But Synge the romantic atheist must have responded deeply to the meaningless but awesome universe Loti draws, in which prayers are not answered, clouds take up certain shapes only because they must take up some shape, wives keep vigil by granite crosses on rocky promontories for husbands who will never return, and even the attitude of the Crucified himself is finally equated to the gesture of a drowning man.

Synge left Paris at the end of April, had a painful interview with Cherrie Matheson in Dublin, and went straight on to Aran; he must have carried with him a heavy freight of moods, ideas and expectations.* His diary for the 10th of May reads simply: 'Dans le batteau à Arranmore à l'Hotel.' The grandly named Atlantic Hotel was a small two-storey building on the quayfront in Cill Rónáin. From there he explored east and west along the road, and then on the third day of his visit he crossed the ridge of the island to the tall cliffs that confront the vastness of the Atlantic. Reliving this experience later on, his notebook gropes among impossible scenarios for a simile:

> I look now backwards to the morning a few weeks ago when I looked first unexpectedly over the higher cliffs of Aranmor, and stopped trembling with delight. A so sudden gust beauty is a danger. It is well arranged that for the most part we do not realize the beauty of a new wonderful experience till it has

---

* This account of his visits to Aran is based on Synge's diaries and notebooks in the manuscripts department of Trinity College Dublin. The fullest of the notebooks (4385), used on his first visit and corresponding to the first and longest section of *The Aran Islands*, has been usefully transcribed by Marek van der Kamp ('An Authentic Aran Journal', M. Phil. thesis, TCD, 1988). On Synge's second visit he used some pages from a notebook (4384) started years earlier in Paris. I have referred to 4385 and 4384 as the first and second notebooks respectively. A third notebook (4387) contains mainly folklore material used in Part IV of his book, and a fourth (4397) also has some notes from his fourth visit.

grown familiar and so safer to us. If a man could be supposed to come with a fully educated perception of music, yet quite ignorant of it and hear for the first time let us say Lamoureux's Orchestra in a late symphony of Beethoven I doubt his brain would ever recover from the shock. If a man could come with a full power of appreciation and stand for the first time before a woman – a woman perhaps who was very beautiful – what would he suffer? If a man grew up knowing nothing of death or decay and found suddenly a corpse in his path what would he suffer? Some such emotion was in me the day I looked first on these magnificent waves towering in dazzling white and green before the cliff.

Strangely, this revelation, equivalent to an instantaneous initiation into art, love and mortality, is not reported in *The Aran Islands* itself. But that slow-acting shock echoes in diminuendo through the four sections of the book, and is re-echoed more distantly in his subsequent works.

In Cill Rónáin Synge got to know an old blind man, Máirtín Ó Conghaile ('Martin Conneely') who had been a guide to George Petrie, Sir William Wilde and others, and who he realized was therefore one of those fabulous Araners he had read of in Petrie 'years since when I was first touched with antiquarian passion'. This living antiquity gave him some lessons in the Irish of Aran, which Synge must have found very different from the Irish he had learned at Trinity, and showed him some of the island's Christian sites, including the late medieval chapel 'of the four beautiful saints' whose holy well was to become the source of his play *The Well of the Saints*.

While in Árainn Synge called on the Church of Ireland minister Mr Kilbride and the Catholic parish priest Fr Farragher, and acquired a camera from a fellow visitor. After a fortnight, finding that Cill Rónáin had been dragged out of the Middle Ages by the Congested Districts Board and become as banal as any other little west-coast fishing village, he left it for Inis Meáin. There he stayed in the MacDonnchas' cottage, and their son Máirtín (Synge calls him Michael in his book) became his guide and tutor. Synge lived for a month on this more primitive island, and also briefly visited Inis Oírr. He spent his time drowsing on the walls of the great cashel that looms over the cottages, wandering with Máirtín or alone, taking photographs* of the islanders (photographs mysteriously in tune with the moods of his prose), and picking up folktales and anecdotes, including those that were to grow into *The Shadow of the Glen* and *The Playboy of the Western World*. Twenty-seven years old and unlucky in love, he was very aware of the beauty of the Aran girls; in his luggage was Loti's account of one of his escapades of Cytherian imperialism, set in Tahiti, *Le mariage de Loti*. He read a lot; other books listed in his diary include Maeterlinck's *Le Tresor des humbles*, *Les grands initiés* by Édouard Scheuré (an admirer of Rudolf Steiner), an unspecified work of Swedenborg's, Rossetti's poems, the Irish mystical poet AE's latest collection *The Earth Spirit*, and, as if as an astringent corrective to these spiritual effusions, Flaubert's *Madame Bovary* and de Maupassant's *Une Vie*, both of them demonstrations of the proposition that (to quote the latter) 'l'être moral de chacun de nous reste éternellement seul par la vie'. And above all, he wrote. A frequent entry in his laconic diary is the single word 'Écrit'. Some at least of this writing was done in little notebooks that would fit into the palm of the hand and that he could use outdoors. It is curiously moving to read, in the stillness of the manuscripts room of Trinity College Dublin, the first connected passage in these notebooks:

> I am laid on the outstretched gable of a cliff and many feet below me great blue waves hurl from time to time a spray that rises in to my face . . . So much spray is in the air that a soft crust forms on the pages of the notebook where I write.

During this first visit Synge witnessed and photographed one of the last – if not the last – eviction raids to be made on the island.† His description of it in *The Aran Islands* is a fine piece of engaged reportage; when he writes

---

*The twenty-three surviving photographs of Aran have been published in *My Wallet of Photographs: The Photographs of J. M. Synge*, arranged and introduced by Lilo Stephens (Dublin, 1971).

† For the background to these evictions, see note 23 on p. 143.

For these people the outrage to the hearth is the supreme catastrophe; they live here in a world of grey, where there are wild
rains and mists every week in the year, and their warm chimney
corners, filled with children and young girls, grow into the
consciousness of each family in a way it is not easy to understand
in more civilized places . . .

he had already shared such a hearth for long enough to intuit
its mysteries. But he also knew about evictions, in their legal
and tactical aspects, from the other side, for his brother
Edward was a professional agent to big landlords and an ef-
ficient practitioner of the art. Synge had had arguments with
his mother on the subject, and when he describes an Aran
mother cursing her son for acting as bailiff in this eviction,
one could imagine Synge's mother rising opposite her to
berate her own son for betraying his class by siding with
rent-defaulting peasants.

On his way back to Dublin, Synge stayed for a few days
at Coole Park, Lady Gregory's home in south Galway, at
Yeats's suggestion. Yeats, Lady Gregory and Edward
Martyn, her neighbour at Tulira Castle, were then planning
the foundation of the Irish Literary Theatre, which later
became the Irish National Theatre. One of the two plays with
which the new venture was inaugurated in May 1899, Yeats's
symbolic drama *The Countess Cathleen*, excited the anger and
incomprehension of the Catholic Church as well as of the
Gaelic League, and the boos with which it was greeted foretold the theatre's turbulent future, on which Synge was to
ride to his own troubled fame.

Synge visited Inis Meáin for nearly a month in September
1899, finding the island, in the rains and storms of autumn, a
darker place, and the islanders dejected after a poor season's
fishing. He caught a feverish cold and had fears of dying and
being buried there before anyone on the mainland could know
of it. He was there again for a month in September of the
following year, when he participated in the islanders' grief
over a drowning and witnessed scenes of despair and resignation out of which he was to make *Riders to the Sea*. Throughout
his Aran seasons he advanced in island proficiencies; he talked

and understood more Irish, learned to row a currach, contributed to evenings of fun and music. He went over to Inis Oírr again for a few days during this third trip; he got to know two girls there, one of whom corresponded with him later on. Whether it was one of these of whom in his notebook he wrote, 'One woman has interested me in a way that binds me more than ever to the islands' is not known; the relationship, whatever its nature, seems to have come to nothing – but one wonders if later on this woman ever felt she had lost the only Playwright of the Western World?

In his alternative life in Paris he was engaged in another profitless love, with an American art student, Margaret Hardon, whom his diary often refers to as 'La Robe Verte'; he sketched a play (later entitled *When the Moon Has Set*) in which a writer loves a nun, whom he persuades to renounce her vows; she exchanges her habit for a green dress and gives herself to him. Reality was not so complaisant, nor was the sketch a success, and Lady Gregory and Yeats when they read it suggested he turn to peasant themes.

By the summer of 1901 Synge had put together the first three parts of his Aran book, which he sent to Lady Gregory; she and Yeats were impressed by it, but thought it would benefit from the inclusion of more fairylore. In late September he revisited Inis Meáin and Inis Oírr for a total of nineteen days. In Inis Meáin several people were ill with typhus, and Synge was horrified at the thought of them dying without a doctor. He would have met the islands' district nurse in Inis Oírr on one of his previous visits – she was later to write a gruesome account of her struggle against the insanitary folk-cures and the filth of those hearthsides Synge found so cherishing* – but it seems that no medical help was available in Inis Meáin at this time. In Inis Oírr he collected folksongs with the dedication of a professional, and translated an eighteenth-century version of the ancient legend, *The Children of Uisneach*, which had been published recently; it was to furnish the matter of his last play, *Deirdre of the Sorrows*.

* B. N. Hedderman, *Glimpses of My Life in Aran*, Part I (Bristol, 1917).

On his way to Paris that November, Synge delivered the manuscript of *The Aran Islands* to a London publisher Yeats had suggested, Grant Allen, who soon returned it. In January 1902 Fisher Unwin, also of London, similarly declined it. His writing career was depressingly unsuccessful; he was still living on an allowance of '£40 a year and a new suit when I am too shabby'. But he doggedly pursued his commitment to the Celtic by following a course in Old Irish at the Sorbonne, where he was frequently the lecturer's sole hearer. These were his seasons of endurance, and they were at last rewarded by a creative outflow; during the next summer, which he spent with his mother in a rented house in Wicklow, he wrote *The Shadow of the Glen* and *Riders to the Sea*, and began *The Tinker's Wedding*. The two completed plays were very welcome to Yeats and Lady Gregory, for their Irish National Theatre was more blessed with talented actors than with plays worth acting. Synge spent twenty-five days in Inis Oírr in October but did not visit Inis Meáin; it was his last trip to the islands and was not reflected in his already completed book.

Synge gave up his Paris apartment that winter and lodged in London, where he was introduced by Lady Gregory and Yeats to the literary world. John Masefield took note of this new, but not young and rather sombre face:

> Something in his air gave one the fancy that his face was dark from gravity. Gravity filled the face and haunted it, as though the man behind were forever listening to life's case before passing judgement ... The face was pale, the cheeks were rather drawn. In my memory they were rather seamed and old-looking. The eyes were at once smoky and kindling. The mouth, not well seen below the moustache, had a great play of humour on it.*

Then he returned to Ireland, and in June 1903 he heard *The Shadow of the Glen* read by Lady Gregory to the actors of the Irish National Theatre. That autumn he visited Kerry instead

*J. Masefield, 'John M. Synge', *The Contemporary Review*, April 1911.

of Aran, and found there an English-speaking peasantry whose dialect he could more immediately adopt into his plays.

The first performance, in October of that year, of *The Shadow of the Glen* was hissed by an audience which pronounced its theme an offence to Irish womanhood. Arthur Griffith, founder of the nationalist organization Sinn Féin and editor of the *United Irishman* newspaper, was particularly violent in his attacks on Synge and the National Theatre. Synge's fantastic realism was at odds with that cast of mind which, tensed in repudiation of the 600-year-long slurs that had accompanied colonization, would admit no defect in the life of Catholic rural Ireland and held that an Irish National Theatre should be the vehicle of patriotic propaganda. His plot had been suggested by a folktale he had heard in Inis Meáin in 1898, concerning a husband who pretends to be dead in order to catch his young wife with her lover; he added to it the wife's abandonment by the pusillanimous lover and her going off with a tramp who has by chance been witness of these events. The setting he chose was one of the great sheep-glens of Wicklow he knew so well. In fact there are sheep everywhere in the dialogue of the play: the productive and individually recognizable sheep of the skilful shepherd who had befriended the lonely wife and then gone mad and died before the action begins, unmanageable sheep escaping in all directions from his incompetent successor the lover, sheep jumping through gaps, leaving their wool on thornbushes, coughing in the fog, stretched out dead with spiders' webs on them, and perhaps even, covertly, aimlessly astray in the famously depressing view from the wife's door, of 'the mists rolling down the bog, and the mists again and they rolling up the bog . . .' Indeed, to accept the nationalists' own simplistic account of why they were disturbed by such a weird drift of disorderly feelings as Synge let loose through this play, is to close one's eyes to the psychological wastes he explores in it.

When *Riders to the Sea*, a sombre presentation of the anguish and resignation of Aran wives and sisters successively robbed by the sea of all their menfolk, was given a first performance in February 1904, it was well received by a small audience, and even Griffith's paper had to admit its tragic beauty. Aran must have long been associated in the public mind with death by drowning; Petrie's account of an old Aran woman still grieving for her son lost to the sea, Burton's painting *The Aran Fisherman's Drowned Child* (exhibited at the Royal Hibernian Academy in 1841, and circulated widely as an engraving*), the heroine's drowning in Emily Lawless's *Grania: The Story of an Island*,† are some earlier treatments of the theme, and Synge's play, the action of which is always on the point of condensing into ritual, was the definitive celebration of the cult. Folk-beliefs of hearth and threshold weigh so heavily if obscurely on speech and gesture in this play that the air its protagonists displace seems thickened with symbol and significance. North, south, east and west are so compulsively evoked as every change of tide and wind brings in new anxiety or despair, that the island itself seethes in a doomful infusion of the compass rose. The elegiac rhythms of Synge's dialogue are those inherent in the English of native Irish speakers, an English the grammar of which has been metamorphosed by the pressure of Irish, and the words of which have therefore been galvanized into new life by syntactic shock. As (necessarily simplified) examples: Irish has two verbal forms that both have to be translated by parts of the verb 'to be' in English; *is*, used in identifying two things, and *tá*, used in attributing a quality to something; thus '*Is é Beartla atá ann*' translates literally as 'It is Bartley that is in it (i.e., there)'. Again, there is no word for 'yes' in Irish; instead one repeats the verb of the question: 'Is it Bartley that is there?' 'It is.' Both these features involve repetition, and thus the possibility of rhythm, when imitated in English. Also, Irish is rich in little tags and

---

* Marie Bourke, *Painting in Focus: 'The Aran Fisherman's Drowned Child' by Frederick William Burton* (Dublin, 1987).

† The Hon. Emily Lawless (1845–1913), daughter of Lord Cloncurry, published her best-known novel *Grania: The Story of an Island*, set in Aran, in 1892; her other works include poetry, historical studies and biography. Synge read *Grania* during his first visit to Aran, and in his notebook criticized the superficiality of her knowledge of the islands.

pieties that prolong a sentence soothingly. Synge calls on all these effects for the simple, death-hushed syllables of this exchange, when the body of one of the drowned sons is brought in:

> Is it Bartley it is?
> It is, surely, God rest his soul.

Here he has avoided the form 'Is it Bartley that's in it?' which in a lighter context he would have exploited. But where there is poetic advantage in it, he will translate word for word, ignoring dictionary equivalents: in '... no one to keen him but the black hags that do be flying on the sea', those ominous and mysterious 'black hags' come literally from the Irish name of the shag or green cormorant, *cailleach dhubh*. And where poetry would be irrecuperably lost, he does not translate at all: in 'the dark nights after Samhain', the Irish word for November is so much more expressive of wind and rain (the pronunciation being approximately 'sawain') and the reminder of the ghosts of Hallowe'en, *Oíche Shamhna*, so much more immediate, that Synge chooses to rely on an Irish audience's familiarity with the word and its associations, and on an English audience's intuition of mystery. Douglas Hyde, in his translations of folksongs, and Lady Gregory in her versions of legends, had preceded Synge in the literary exploration of the borderzone between Irish and English inhabited by the folk-people of Ireland, but Synge is the only playboy of this western world of words, in which he grew to his full freedom and power. Synge's language is the translation into English not of an Irish text but of the Irish language itself.

The company went on to a great success in London with Synge's two plays, especially *Riders to the Sea*. In that summer of 1904 it took over what was to become the Abbey Theatre, leased through the generosity of an English admirer of Yeats, Miss Horniman, and rehearsals of *The Well of the Saints* soon began. Synge visited Kerry again, and then, instead of going to Aran as planned, took his bicycle down to Belmullet in the far west of Mayo. This extraordinarily bleak and remote peninsula was to become the setting for *The Playboy of the Western*

World, although he had picked up the germ of its plot in Inis Meáin.

The Well of the Saints was performed in February 1905, and evoked the same rage in nationalist quarters as had *The Shadow of the Glen*. Indeed this grim and comic morality of uncaring youth and foolish age, in which even sanctity and miracle appear as tactless intrusions into hard-won if fantasizing accommodations with reality, holds little comfort for anyone. The setting is again Wicklow, but the well of the title, from which a roving saint has brought holy water to cure an old blind couple, is the one Synge visited in Árainn in company with old Martin Conneely. He could have heard tales of such cures told of any of hundreds of holy wells throughout Ireland, but perhaps in the dreamworkmanship of creativity there was a link between his plot – of old Martin Doul (*dall*, 'blind') and his wife being cured of their blindness, regretting it when they discover they are not the beautiful couple they had imagined, and slowly recovering their blindness – and the odd fact of Synge's being shown a well reputed to cure blindness, by a blind man.

In *Riders to the Sea* the young curate is dismissed near the beginning of the play as powerless to avert the impending tragedy, and the comforts of official doctrine are nowhere called upon in its aftermath; the miracle-worker of *The Well of the Saints* sees his dissatisfied clients stumble off to make their own way through a dangerous world by the light of their own darkness; similarly, in *The Tinker's Wedding*, which Synge was working on at this time, the wanderers of earth finally assert the irrelevance of the clergy to their lifecycles: 'it's little need we ever had of the like of you to get us our bit to eat, and our bit to drink, and our time of love when we were young men and women and were fine to look at'. Synge's tribute to the born anarchs of the Wicklow roads whom he appreciated so much was never staged in his lifetime. The rejection of religious authority implicit in most of his work was acted out in this play, in which the tinkers bundle the venal priest into a sack when he refuses to marry them without his 'dues' being paid in full. In his preface to the text, published in 1907, Synge hopes that the country people, from tinkers to clergy, would not mind being laughed at without malice, but at the time Yeats was not so optimistic; he felt the play would cause too much trouble for his young theatre, and Synge seems to have agreed. The first performance of it took place in London in 1909, after Synge's death, and it was not seen in Ireland until the year of the Synge Centenary Commemoration, 1971.

In 1905, at the prompting of Masefield, the *Manchester Guardian* commissioned Synge to write a series of articles on the distressed state of the Congested Districts. The artist Jack Yeats, younger brother of the poet, was to illustrate the articles, and the two of them explored Connemara and Belmullet that summer. On his return Synge wrote to MacKenna:

> Unluckily my commission was to write on the 'Distress' so I couldn't do anything like what I would have wished as an interpretation of the whole life ... There are sides of all that western life the groggy-patriot-publican-general shop-man who is married to the priest's half sister and is second cousin once-removed of the dispensary doctor, that are horrible and awful ... I sometimes wish to God I hadn't a soul and then I could give myself up to putting those lads on the stage. God, wouldn't they hop! In a way it is all heartrending, in one place the people are starving but wonderfully attractive and charming and in another place where things are going well one has a rampant double-chinned vulgarity I haven't seen the like of.*

This is impercipient, as personal and business relationships in the small towns of western Ireland were not more incestuous than in Synge's own family or artistic milieus; but then a substantial stratum of Irish life hardly found expression in the works of the Irish cultural revival, which recognized no muse between the ranks of countess and colleen. However, the imposed theme focused his eyes on the miserable obverse of the rural economics that had delighted him in Aran, and he expressed this darker matter of poverty and exploitation with moving directness. The articles were republished after his death in the 1910 edition of his works, despite Yeats's feeling

* *The Collected Letters of John Millington Synge*, ed. Ann Saddlemyer, 2 vols. (Oxford, 1983).

that they were inferior. Jack Yeats was later to illustrate the first (1907) edition of *The Aran Islands* with twelve drawings, some of them evidently based on Synge's photographs and only one or two of them remotely adequate to the subtle and vigorous text.

Synge had been engaged in the tempestuous politics of the Irish National Theatre from its foundation, and in the autumn of 1905 he became one of its three directors, with Yeats and Lady Gregory; as he explained in a letter to MacKenna, Yeats looked after the stars while he saw to everything else. Soon afterwards a number of the more politically oriented actors seceded, and among those brought in to replace them was a nineteen-year-old girl, Molly Allgood, with whom Synge was soon in love. He had been living with his mother – for their close relationship still persisted despite her incomprehension of his work – but now he took rooms in the suburbs of Dublin, both to be nearer his theatre and to see more of Molly. She was a cheerful and comparatively uneducated girl whose frank enjoyment of such innocent treats as picnics with other members of the company came to torment the jealous and serious-minded Synge; his Dublin Albertine used to annotate his multitudinous, obsessive and insinuating letters with brisk one-word judgements: 'idiotic', or 'peculiar', or 'frivolous'. She was also a Roman Catholic, which promised to cause consternation in his family when their affair should become known. But she inspired the love-talk of Synge's most richly realized character, Christy Mahon of *The Playboy of the Western World*. Synge wrote the part of Pegeen Mike in that play with Molly in mind, and she played that role in the first performance in January 1907.

The company were anxious about the wildly prodigal language of the play, and presented it to their highly reactive audience with trepidation. Yeats was in Scotland at the time, and after Act Two had been received with attention Lady Gregory sent him a telegram: 'Play great success.' But Act Three provoked such an uproar that she sent off another telegram: 'Audience broke up in disorder at the word shift.' The 'Playboy Riots' were to become part of theatrical legend. As

Synge wrote to Molly the next morning, 'Now we'll be talked about. We're an event in the history of the Irish stage. I have a splitting headache ...' Large numbers of police – the Royal Irish Constabulary, to the nationalists an arm of foreign oppression – were called upon to preserve a semblance of order for the following performances, which were largely inaudible. Yeats returned hastily from Scotland, lectured the baying crowd from the stage with courage and dignity, went into court to testify against arrested rioters, and within a few days organized a public debate, in which despite personal reservations he spoke himself hoarse for Synge's play against a tumultuous audience. Synge himself was at home in bed suffering from exhaustion and influenza.

The story of the *Playboy* had been developed out of two incidents Synge had heard of in the west: one, of a Connemara man who murdered his father and was sheltered by the people of Inis Meáin for a while, supplied the theme of parricide, and the other, of a Mayo man who assaulted the lady he was employed by, repeatedly escaped from custody, taunted the police in letters and was protected by various lady-friends, added the ingredients of sexual attractiveness and verbal dexterity.* Griffith in an editorial described the play as 'a vile

---

*Synge mentions the story of the Connemara man hidden by the islanders in Part I of *The Aran Islands* (p. 50), and in a draft of this passage he adds, 'Another story is told here of a highway robber who escaped from his prison and hid himself away among the people in the Connaught hills ... At last two girls were arrested on a charge of harbouring him, and he gave himself up to clear them. This happened recently.' The Connemara man was the son of a poor farmer called Ó Máille and was born about 1838 in Callow, west of Roundstone, where his story is not quite forgotten. According to local lore collected early in this century (Tomás Ó Máille, *An Ghaoth Aniar*, Dublin, 1920), he was a handsome athletic man, the pride of the neighbourhood, but his father was a quarrelsome drunkard. When the son wanted to plant some potatoes, the father tried to stop him by grabbing his 'loy', or spade, and in the struggle had an attack and seemed about to die. Young Ó Máille took to the hills and, after eluding the police for several months, crossed to Cill Rónáin (current tradition is that he was smuggled in a barrel on to a boat in Clifden harbour) where he was sheltered by a woman relative (who it seems was still living next door to the Atlantic Hotel at the time of Synge's visits). Because he was so distressed by what he had done, and was talking to nobody, the islanders

and inhuman story told in the foulest language we have ever listened to from a public platform'. While it is clear that audiences came to the play primed by such opinions to be shocked, it should be recognized that *The Playboy of the Western World* is genuinely shocking. We, nine shocking decades later, if we are not rattled to our ontologies by a play, tend to want our money back; but it is hardly surprising that those unhardened Dublin audiences, facing such a flood of bizarre talk and action bursting from depths in which tragic, including Oedipal, themes echo like laughter, found it difficult even to pinpoint the source of their disquiet. When Christy at the peak of passion cries, 'It's Pegeen I'm seeking only, and what'd I care if

---

tried to cheer him up with parties, dances and cardgames. Word of his presence reached the authorities, so the islanders took him to Inis Meáin, and when the police surrounded the cottage in which he was sheltering there the man of the house let himself be captured in his place. After living rough for a time, Ó Máille got away to Tralee in a boat carrying potatoes from Árainn and signed on as a sailor in a ship for America. He revisited Galway as a ship's captain two years later.

The other case was that of James Lynchehaun (*c.* 1858–*c.* 1937), a wild and unpredictable school-teacher who had already been arrested for a minor assault and jumped bail before the period of the crime that made him famous. In 1894 he was facing eviction by Mrs Agnes MacDonnell of Achill Island, Co. Mayo, who had been his employer. Her stables burned down one night and during the confusion she was assaulted and left dreadfully battered, with her nose nearly bitten off. Later that night her house burned down as well. She accused Lynchehaun of the assault (and he was probably behind the burnings too). He was arrested, escaped from the police, was hidden by distant relatives including a young female cousin, in a hole in their floor under a dresser, was discovered and rearrested, tried and condemned to life imprisonment. He became celebrated in ballads and in newspaper reports as 'the Achill troglodyte'. In 1902 he made a most ingenious and daring escape from Maryborough Gaol and got away to America. When arrested there he claimed his crime was political, and with the support of the Irish nationalist community avoided deportation. He revisited Achill in disguise in 1907 and returned safely to America, despite having been briefly detained by the local police over a break-in. Later he returned to Achill again, was arrested and released after a few months. It seems he died in Girvan, Scotland. In *The Playboy* he is mentioned as 'the man bit the yellow lady's nostril'. 'Yellow' here means English, as in the derogatory Irish name for an Englishman, *Sean Buí*, 'yellow John'; Mrs MacDonnell had English connections. (See James Carney, *The Playboy and the Yellow Lady*, Swords, Co. Dublin, 1986.)

you brought me a drift of chosen females, standing in their shifts itself, maybe, from this place to the eastern world?' they thought they found the word 'shift' offensive as being an indelicate synonym of 'chemise'; in fact it is the steam-hiss of an exorbitant fantasy compressed into a moment. Synge, to some degree, knew what he was at. As he wrote to MacKenna, 'On the French stage you get sex without its balancing elements: on the Irish stage you get the other elements without the sex. I restored sex and people were so surprised they saw the sex only.'

The play was taken to England in the summer, and although Yeats decided that it was too risky to put it on in Birmingham where what he called 'the slum Irish' might have been organized by the nationalists to demonstrate against it, performances in Oxford and London were very successful. Synge was in London and in good health for the occasion, and was lionized. Also *The Aran Islands* had at last been published (by Elkin Mathews in London and Maunsel in Dublin), and so 1907 gave him his brief summer of glory. July he spent in the Wicklow hills; Molly and her sister came to spend a fortnight at a cottage near his, and they rambled and rejoiced together.

Over the next autumn he worked on a play very different from his four savage comedies. The plot of his tragedy *Deirdre of the Sorrows* is adapted from an ancient Irish tale, a version of which he had translated in Inis Oírr five years before: the lovely girl being brought up in seclusion as bride for the old king who rules at Emain persuades the young huntsman she has seen in the woods to run away with her, but eventually returns to Emain and the fate foretold at her birth, as if compelled by the beauty of her own legend. Although Synge's setting is of woods and hillsides, references to the clouds coming from the west and south, and the rain since the night of Samhain, soon take us back to the meteorological determinism of *Riders to the Sea*. Deirdre appears at first as the child of nature itself, unpossessable by all the knowledge and power of civilization, and ends in suicide over a grave dug in the earth, mourned by nature: 'if the oaks and stars could die for sorrow, it's a dark sky and a hard and naked earth we'd have this night in Emain'. Perhaps this is the echo of that thunderous revelation, transcending art, love and death, on the cliffs of Árainn; long-delayed, almost too long-delayed . . .

For Synge's period of incipient glory was also that of his dying, and *Deirdre of the Sorrows* was never to be quite finished. His neck glands had been troublesome for some time, and in September he had been operated on for their removal. Although he still discussed marriage plans with Molly, and revisited Kerry, his periods of health and good spirits were sporadic now, and there were endless quarrels and schisms within the theatre company to depress him further. His family no longer opposed his marriage, but it had to be postponed when he went into hospital in April 1908 for investigation of a painful lump in his side, and was found to have an inoperable tumour. He was not told of the fatal implications, and for a time felt much better, but the pain returned. The household he was preparing for Molly had to be broken up, and he returned to live with his mother, who was failing too. Writing to Molly, he said, 'She seems quite a little old woman with an old woman's voice. It makes me sad. It is sad also to see all *our* little furniture stored away in these rooms. It is a sad queer time for us all, dear Heart, I sometimes feel inclined to sit down and wail.' Then, rallying, he went off to Oberwerth to see the Von Eiken sisters once again, and bought works by the medieval German poets von der Vogelweide and Hans Sachs with the intention of translating them. His mother died while he was still in Germany, and he did not feel well enough to face the journey home for her funeral. On his return he lived alone in his mother's house, and worked intermittently on his *Deirdre*. He looked through his earlier work and wrote,

> I read about the Blaskets and Dunquin,
> The Wicklow towns and fair days I've been in.
> I read of Galway, Mayo, Aranmore,
> And men with kelp along a wintry shore.
> Then I remembered that that 'I' was I,
> And I'd a filthy job – to waste and die.

By the spring the filthy job was done. He entered Elpis Hospital again on the 2nd of February 1909 and died there on the 24th of March. At the funeral, his family and his artistic colleagues formed two immiscible groups, and the fisherfolk, tramps and playboys of Ireland of course knew nothing of it.

THE BOOK

> Kilronan . . . has been so much changed by the fishing industry, developed there by the Congested Districts Board, that it now has very little to distinguish it from any fishing village on the west coast of Ireland. The other islands are more primitive, but even on them many changes are being made, that it was not worth while to deal with in the text.

Thus Synge in his brief introduction divides Aran into the primitive and the not worth writing about. His text, though, overflows his programme. In fact on his typescript* Synge scribbled, '*Note* If the early chapters explain themselves I would prefer m.s. without any Introduction. J.M.S.' Obviously the publishers' worldly wisdom prevailed, but in ideality Synge was right: all introductions (and introductory essays by third persons) by indicating a perspective reduce the dimensionality of what they introduce, and so should be read only after the work itself – but by the time one realizes this, it is too late. Synge lent his European mind to Aran for a while on generously indefinite terms, and *The Aran Islands* can be read in many ways. A sentence in Synge's second notebook insists on one: 'I cannot say it too often, the supreme interest of the island lies in the strange concord that exists between the people and the impersonal limited but powerful impulses of the nature that is round them' – and so the essential matter of the book is an ecology of moods. Later on he took a more distanced view (and one can trace this growing detachment in the book itself, as the divergences of the islanders from his prescription of them become their most interesting and theatrically engaging aspect, and a relish for the actual quarrels in him with his thirst for the ideal); in 1907 he wrote to a friend, 'I look on

---

*The typescript, together with an earlier draft, is no. 4344 of the Synge manuscripts in TCD Library.

The Aran Islands as my first serious piece of work ... In writing out the talk of the people and their stories in this book, and in a certain number of articles on the Wicklow peasantry which I have not yet collected, I learned to write the peasant dialect and dialogue which I use in my plays.' So the book is a stage in the evolution of Synge the dramatist. It has also been read in a sociolinguistic mode as 'fictionalized confessional autobiography'* and can be seen as a set of symptoms of the dilemmas of the late nineteenth-century Anglo-Irish mind. Books shed meanings as trees their leaves, year after year, in their slow growth and maturation. Nearly a century has passed since Synge first walked the bare wet rocks of Aran and his old blind guide put the riddle of the Sphinx to him. That double-natured and sphinx-like creature, Synge-on-Aran, still proposes its riddle, which is that of our own mortal stance on the earth. Now that our planet has shrunk to an island in space (if not to a Congested District, and with no fatherly Board set over it!), all past efforts to unriddle our being-on-the-earth have to be reread; perhaps Synge's book will reach another maturity in this age of secular eschatologies.

The Aran Islands is in four parts, corresponding to the first four of his five visits. At the start he materializes, as it were, out of rain and fog on to the big island, Árainn, and meets a satisfactorily medieval mentor who talks of women carried off by fairies and gives him scraps of lore in which the Celtic hero Diarmaid and Samson from the Bible cohere with classical motifs, as in the detrital culture of the hedge-schools. But he is surprised at the fluency and abundance of 'the foreign tongue', i.e. his own language, in Cill Rónáin, and only a few pages after his arrival he removes to Inis Meáin, having come to the conclusion that life there 'is perhaps the most primitive in Europe'. The first sentence of the Inis Meáin pages echoes the first sentence of the book so closely as to give the impression that the latter merely represented a false start and that it is only now that we are really beginning:

* Mary C. King, *The Drama of John Millington Synge* (London, 1985).

> I am settled at last on Inishmaan in a small cottage with a
> continual drone of Gaelic coming from the kitchen that opens
> into my room.

We acquire two meagre hints about Synge's non-Aran existence in these preliminary pages. An old islander tells him that
he recognized his likeness to his relative who was in Aran
forty-three years earlier – and so we learn of the Synge connection with the islands from the lips of an Aran man, not from
the author's. The fact that Synge's uncle was the Protestant
incumbent is not stated. And on the trip across to Inis Meáin,
his crew call out to some comrades that they 'had a man with
them who had been in France a month from this day'. Again,
we learn a fact about Synge through its reflection (as a wonder)
in the minds of the islanders. Thus one of the book's principles
of exclusion is early established, and is only underlined by the
very occasional subsequent reference to Paris, standing for all
that is not Aran. Another of these principles may be induced
from the fact that most of the folktales he records are dropped
into the text without comment, as they would have cropped up
in Aran life, in the course of a conversational walk or an evening's entertainment. Only in the case of the first tale he heard
in Inis Meáin, about the man who bets on his wife's faithfulness
during his absence, does he permit himself a belletristic ex-
cursus on its European antecedents: 'the gay company who
went out from Florence to tell narratives of love', 'the *Pecorone*
of Ser Giovanni, a Florentine notary', and so on. The passage
has been praised for its skilful condensation of an extensive
body of literary lore, but it does not convince one that it was
written out of Synge's memory in Inis Meáin, and as a flaw in
the appearance of immediacy that controls the rest of the book,
it is the one false note in the whole. (The fourth and last
section of the book is perhaps even overloaded with this folk
material, which, though interesting in itself, is not fully thought
into the texture of the work.) Thus, by opposites as it were, a
specification of the book's content is implied; it is the content
of the mind of a visitor on the island, not of someone writing
about the island from a study on the mainland.

There are other principles of exclusion at work too. A comparison of the contents of his notebooks and the finished work tells much about the rigour of Synge's processes of composition. For instance, a much revised version of the passage about the spray on the leaves of the notebook itself, quoted above (p. xxiv), is found in a draft of *The Aran Islands*, but it does not occur in the finished work. As it in fact relates to the cliffs on the big island, this, like other omissions, seems to indicate that Synge wanted to truncate his account of the big island and hasten his definitive settling in Inis Meáin. This same passage in the draft is conflated with some inept nature-notes from the first notebook:

> Everything in Aran has a certain rarity or distinction. Dandelion and buttercup here have yielded up their place to pansies with pale yellow lips, blackfooted maidenhair – to translate its [Gaelic] epithet – clings to the rock among the bracken and rooks and daws are replaced by these more graceful choughs.

Since dandelions and buttercups are glorious in the islands, the fern called in Irish the 'black foot' is not the maidenhair, etc., Synge's final decision not to treat of the flora is wise; even his very general comment on it (p. 37), 'On these rocks, where there is no growth of animal or vegetable life, all the seasons are the same', is depressingly unobservant – but then it is wafted into a magical and melancholy subjectivity by its conclusion: '– and this June day is so full of autumn that I listen unconsciously for the rustle of dead leaves'. Another entry in the first notebook not reflected in the final work is on Dún Aonghasa:

> The antiquarian treasures of the islands are not strictly in the scope of my scattered notes and they have often been described. Some however possess such conspicuous individual beautiful that they come plainly beneath the impressionist. I have just visited Dun Angus a great primeval fortress placed with strong boldness on the edge of the highest cliff in Aran ... The dull leaden grey of the evening though unlovely in itself was fitted to evoke the sense of absolute loneliness here at home. These races who raised the three great circles of concentric walls, what was their real feeling as they gazed in simple raiment from the cliff where I gazed?

In one of the later drafts this train of thought is continued:

> My sadness and delight are older than the walls about me, and
> have lingered round these rocks since men were hairy and naked,
> for emotion is as inherent a property to this place as the colour
> or odour of the waves.

But the attempt at recuperating the emotions of hairy prehistory by means of the dubious metaphysics of their inherence in the rocks is abandoned, together with the description of the site. In fact Dún Aonghasa is one of the most striking absences in the book, and even the huge cashel lowering over Synge's cottage in Inis Meáin is left undescribed except as 'a corona of stone'.

Most visitors to the islands are as impressed by the great cashels as they are by the luxuriance of the summer flowers; but even before these perceptions they are overawed by the presence of stone everywhere. Synge certainly gives one the picture of a bare and stony island, but his account nowhere conveys the extreme stoniness of Inis Meáin, which is remarkable even in the context of the Aran Islands. Two aspects of this feature have been noted above: the sheets of smooth naked rock that extend for hundreds of yards in terraces below the line of villages, and the mighty stormbeach around the exposed southern shoreline and on top of the western cliffs. Synge does not mention these two astounding formations, which insistently raise the question of geological origins, of the processes of time; it is as if he wanted to generalize his island into elemental simplicity and atemporality. Similarly the striking out of Dún Aonghasa from his record amounts to the suppression of the islands' history. Neither the rich corpus of legends and traditions associated with Aran's saints and monasteries, nor the dramas of the Cromwellian conquest, nor the piteous hungerlore of the Famine century, figure in his account. The great echo-chambers of the past, from the geological birth through the prehistory and history of the islands, are closed off, almost down to the immediately relevant inheritance of landlordism. On the eve of the threatened evictions Synge asks, as if the question had just come into his head, who owns Inis Meáin; and the islanders' answer places the matter in the perspectives of the picturesque: 'Bedad, we always heard it belonged to Miss —, and she is dead.' The islands, then, exist only in the shallow, cyclic time of sunsets and tides and seasons, the rippling weather-like time so accurately metered by Synge's prose style itself. The pathos of this situation, its vulnerability, is expressed in the first of the notebooks, which so often spell out what is left implicit in the book itself:

> The thought that this island will gradually yield to the ruthlessness of 'progress' is as the certainty that decaying age is moving always nearer the cheeks it is your extasy to kiss. How much of Ireland was formerly like this and how much of Ireland is today Anglicized and civilized and brutalized?

All that has happened to our world impends upon his island; the islanders are soon to be evicted from stasis and sent wandering on the roads of history.

Thus some of Synge's omissions merely result from a decision not to be didactic or to waste time in acquiring the low-grade omniscience other topographical writers aspire to, while certain themes broached in the notebooks lead him too far into the personal for exposure in the published work. But the grand exclusions mentioned above are definitive of the work itself, and to note them is not to criticize his creation but to situate it, to discover its co-ordinates, the negative ones as well as the positive, and to measure the richness of its austerity by the stringency of its rejections, the magnitude of the sacrifice of material (self-sacrifice, Synge being so at one with much of this material) necessary to carve it into the form it aspires to, which is island-like, extramundane. But what sort of truth does this drastic paring-away of reality leave to his claim in the introduction that he has written 'a direct account of [his] life on the islands . . . changing nothing that is essential'? The life-currents that bring him repeatedly to the islands and carry him off again are virtually unrepresented in the book, which suggests that progressive, autobiographical time is as irrelevant as history to the truths he is conveying. And in listening for these truths, one has to be aware of variable distances between his islands and the Aran of our geographies, as well as between the visitor he projects on the islands and the Synge of the biographies. Synge the writer, for instance, had to put down thousands of words on that spray-encrusted paper while in Aran; the visitor's mind retains the most complex sensations and intuitions in their pristine perfection.

The boat-trip to Inis Meáin from Cill Rónáin, that awkward compromise of Aran with the mainland, had given that visitor the 'exquisite satisfaction' of moving away from civilization in a canoe of a model that had 'served primitive races since men first went on the sea'. The middle island is the real Aran, and its indubitable rock soon wears out his boots, so the islanders make him a pair of rawhide moccasins like their own in which he learns the 'natural walk of man'. These initiations into the archaic, this casting off of modern life like a worn-out pair of boots, suggest that for Synge our civilization itself is merely something interposed, for the sake of false decency and craven comfort, between us and the harsh and beautiful truths of our world.

The visitor's description of the interior of the cottage he is to lodge in is aglow with the colours of homecoming. He feels that the handmade articles of local materials not only 'give this simple life, where all art is unknown, something of the artistic beauty of medieval life', but seem to be 'a natural link between the people and the world that is about them'. The islanders' way of life, he notes, 'has never been acted on by anything much more artificial than the nests and burrows of the creatures that live round them'. This action on them of the natural, though, is of a Darwinian ruthlessness; great dexterity is needed to bring a currach into land on a rocky shore through the breakers, and 'this continual danger . . . has had considerable influence on the local character, as the waves have made it impossible for clumsy, foolhardy, or timid men to live on these islands'. It is particularly in Part I that Synge builds up this picture of a life lived hand in hand with nature, as, for instance, in his accurate observation of how the appearance of the village street changes with the wind's direction, either all the south doors being open, or all the north doors, and so of how his hostess's ability to judge the time depends on whether or not the sun is casting the shadow of the south door's jamb on the kitchen floor. (How strange it is, that Synge's first gift to his hosts was to be an alarm-clock!) This sympathy between man and nature works both ways, the visitor is forced to believe, after witnessing a burial at which the thunder seems to join in the keening for the dead.

The visitor is not just an observer of the islands' enviable naturalness, but a novitiate; he learns some of their sea-skills, their language. On his second visit he shows the islanders some photographs he took the previous year, and

> a beautiful young woman I had spoken to a few times last year slipped in, and after a wonderfully simple and cordial speech of welcome, she sat down on the floor beside me to look on also. The complete absence of shyness or self-consciousness in most of these people gives them a peculiar charm, and when this young and beautiful woman leaned across my knees to look nearer at some photograph that pleased her, I felt more than ever the strange simplicity of the island life.

Synge's second notebook goes further: 'Another visit is over ... One woman also has interested me in a way that binds me more than ever to the islands. The women are before convention and share many things with the women of Paris and London.' During his first visit he had been reading Pierre Loti, arch-exponent of the temporary marriage both as a form of life and as a literary genre, and had noted for himself, apropos of *Le mariage de Loti*, 'The wanderer has many pains that are known to wanderers only; in a score of places I also have longed to linger for my life and marry me with the woman that has mostly appeared to personify as a central life each new system of sensation.' The personification of the island as a woman comes no doubt from the promptings of a young man's blood as well as from the august precedents of Celtic myths in which the king marries the tutelary goddess of his realm. The notebook is more visceral than anything in the published text: 'With this limestone Inishmaan ... I am in love, and hear with galling jealousy of the various priests and scholars who have lived here before me. They have grown to me as former lovers of one's mistress, horrible existences haunting with dreamed kisses the lips she presses to your own.' By the end of his third season in Aran the visitor is telling the islanders that he is going back to Paris to sell his books and his bed (the elemental furnishings of his life), and then coming back to grow as strong and simple as they among the islands of the west. The next year, in self-ironizing counterpoint to his own romanticism, he also records the advice of the young men to him, that he should marry a fine, fat island girl who would have plenty of children and not be wasting his money on him.

But it is when alone, as he is for long hours, that the visitor enters into his own ecology of Being, finding his introspective way to that oneness with the natural world he divines in the island culture. He begins to understand the island nights and the distinction they lend to those who work by dark; he spends time by himself near the shore in darkness so absolute he cannot see or realize his own body and exists only in his hearing waves and smelling seaweed. He lies on the cliff-edge and experiences something of the revelation of inanimate vastitude Synge tried to express in his first notebook; he seems 'to enter into the wild pastimes of the cliff, and to become a companion of the cormorants and crows'. (A draft for the Aran cliff episode goes further than this Wordsworthian empathy: 'I fulfil a function like the litchen and the grass, and my thoughts are older than the stones about me' – but this illumination is not developed.) And if he were to become part of this island universe, it would at the last treat him with dignity and accept him into its own element: 'This death, with fresh sea salt in one's teeth, would be better than most deaths one is likely to meet' – a thought the first notebook elaborates into a painfully realistic prevision of the death that would face Synge himself: 'to struggle in soiled sheets and thick stifling blankets with the smell of my own illness in my nostrils and a half paid death tender at my side till my long death battle will be fought out'.

Thus three identifications are being asserted: of the islanders with the island, of the visitor with the islanders, and of the island with the visitor. But none of these is without its painful contradictions, and Synge is true to those as well. Sometimes it is the Aran people who do not live up to the vision he has of them. The claim that the waves forbid the existence of clumsy or foolhardy men on the islands is undermined by the anecdote in Part I of a half-drunken crew rowing the visitor 'at an absurd pace' in a currach slowly filling with water from a leak which they had 'with their usual carelessness' neglected to mend. Often the Araners are distracted by the outside world from their island natures: 'Yet it is only in the intonation of a few sentences or some old fragment of melody that I catch the real spirit of the island, for in general the men sit together and talk with endless iteration of the tides and fish, and of the price of kelp in Connemara.' Synge could imagine better Aran men than these, and eventually he had to create his Araners of the mind, in *Riders to the Sea*. At the same time the visitor, in common humanity, cannot but listen sympathetically to the islanders' economic problems. 'The price of kelp in Connemara', in particular, was to be a question of heartrending importance for the Aran Islanders Synge depicted in his 1905 articles on 'the distress' in the Congested Districts, but for the visitor in Aran in 1898 such a question was only an interruption, part of the deplorable but inevitable intrusion of the mainland which was coercing and seducing the islands away from their essence. The most aggressive instance of this coercion is the eviction party of sweaty policemen who contrast so horribly with islanders as cool as seagulls; the most beguiling of the seductions is the shrill handbell calling the womenfolk to a meeting of the Gaelic League. The absurdity of applying mainland law to the seagull-islanders and of charging them rent for the rock they perch on is manifest; the teaching of written Irish is ominous, for it heralds the death of their oral culture and the clogging of their language with the dross of modern life.

But even if the outside world leaves them alone and uncorrupted, can the islanders really be at home in 'a universe that wars on them with winds and seas'? In the last two sections of the book Synge describes repeated scenes of anguish over deaths by drowning, which evidently affected him deeply.*

---

*Synge has been criticized by the anthropologist John C. Messenger not only for 'primitivism' and 'nativism' but for projecting a tragic world vision

The account in Part IV of the woman dying of typhus, while her menfolk row off into mist and wind in a vain quest for help, ends with the visitor talking with the old folk around the fireside of the sorrows of the people until late in the night. Coming from a funeral, he watches fishermen at work with a dragnet on the shore, and feels that they are all under a judgement of death on sea or land, and will all be battered naked on the rocks or buried with another such fearful scene in the graveyard as he has just witnessed. The islanders' symbiotic pact with nature, then, leaves them helpless when it is broken, in the absence of civilization's support.

The visitor's own aspiration to oneness with the island community is problematic too. During his second stay he realizes how far away from him these people are: 'They like me sometimes, and laugh at me sometimes, yet never know what I am doing.' The cultural spaces between him and the islanders seem impassable: 'They have the same emotions that I have, and the animals have, yet I cannot talk to them when there is much to say ... On some days I feel this island as a perfect

---

on island life (*Inis Beag, Isle of Ireland*, New York, 1969; *Inis Beag Revisited*, Salem, Wisconsin, 1989; 'Islanders Who Read', *Anthropology Today*, April 1988). Messenger, in the course of his researches in Inis Oírr in 1959–60, reckoned up that there had been only four sea accidents, with the loss of but twelve lives, in that island since 1850, and states that Synge's claim that every family has lost men to the sea 'reflects not only his masochism but the broadness of kinship reckoning'. Amazingly, the world of Synge scholarship seems meekly to have accepted this rebuke. Quite apart from any too subtle considerations of the exact reality-status of Synge's verbal creation, it should be pointed out that Inis Oírr is another island, and that his remarks on drownings are closely linked to specific incidents – two due to drunkenness in which four lives were lost, a drowning of three men of one family 'a few years ago', the destruction of fishing boats in Killeany Bay, and another loss of a young man whose funeral he attended. Synge also reports the realism of an islander's view of the use of fear: 'A man who is not afraid of the sea will soon be drownded, for he will be going out on a day he shouldn't. But we do be afraid of the sea, and we do only be drownded now and again.' And when that 'now and again' comes, which is the more adequate response, the anthropologist's statistics or Synge's prose, as resonant as the keening of the grief-stricken relatives?

home and resting place; on other days I feel that I am a waif among the people.' And (in Part IV) it is not just he himself with his insufficient Irish who is excluded, but the whole civilization that he was born into: 'I became indescribably mournful, for I felt this little corner on the face of the world, and the people who live in it, have a peace and dignity from which we are shut for ever.' Similarly his attempts at direct communion with the island itself can lead him into dark moods:

> After a few hours [of walking in the storm] the mind grows bewildered with the endless change and struggle of the sea, and an utter despondency replaces the first moment of exhilaration ... The wind is terrific. If anything serious should happen to me I might die here and be nailed in my box, and shoved down into a wet crevice in the graveyard before any one could know it on the mainland.

Here is the bad death, grim alternative to the heroic sea-change he had proposed for himself as an Aran currach-man, during his first rhapsodic immersion in island life.

From his early days in Inis Meáin the visitor records a striking dream, in which he is seduced into an ecstatic dance by music tuned to a forgotten scale, that becomes a vortex annihilating all outside itself and changes suddenly to shrieking agony. The dream hardly bears the theory it is burdened with: 'Some dreams I have had in this cottage seem to give strength to the opinion that there is a psychic memory attached to certain places' – which reads like a perfunctory nod to Yeats.* Synge's mind was too positivistic to entertain the mysticism of AE's *The Earth Breath* either (and he confesses in the first notebook that he is too profane and sophisticated to see 'the small gentry' with which the islanders' island is swarming at night). If this dream represents the blissful and deadly dance of union with nature, it also enacts the rebellion of the individual intelligence against such pantheistic self-obliteration.

* In view of this theory it is odd that the only dream Synge's diary records from Aran was of a riot in connection with the Dreyfus case, which was agitating Paris at the time.

Thus it seems that there is a painful contradiction between the necessity and the impossibility of each of three identifications constituting wholeness, between the visitor, the islanders and the island itself – or between the individual, the community and the natural world, if we may read by the light of the question Synge asks himself in his notebook, on taking leave of the island after his first rapturous appropriation of it: 'In this ocean, is not every symbol of the cosmos?' And it is on the site defined by this triangle of tragic conflicts that Synge, in one sentence near its beginning, conjures the spirit of his book:

> The continual passing in this island between the misery of last night and the splendour of today, seems to create an affinity between the moods of these people and the moods of varying rapture and dismay that are frequent in artists, and in certain forms of alienation.

Here the island, the islanders and the writer are as one, subject to the manic-depressive regime of the Atlantic. It is the swift and transitionless alternations of emotional weather that give his book its characteristic texture, and this is no mere surface phenomenon or stylistic finish, but a structure deeper than the fourfold division of the work or of any analysis of it by themes. This structure expresses itself in miniature in the exquisite portrait of a young island girl whom he salutes across the chasms that divide them, as a kindred soul:

> As we sit on stools on either side of the fire I hear her voice going backwards and forwards in the same sentence from the gaiety of a child to the plaintive intonation of an old race that is worn with sorrow. At one moment she is a simple peasant, at another she seems to be looking out at the world with a sense of prehistoric disillusion and to sum up in the expression of her grey-blue eyes the whole external despondency of the clouds and the sea.

In this passage we are surely looking into the face of Synge's Aran herself.

Tim Robinson
Connemara 1991

Acknowledgements

I am grateful to the following for their advice and expertise in various fields: Professor Tomás de Bhaldraithe (Royal Irish Academy), W. J. Mc Cormack (Department of English, Trinity College Dublin), Dónall Mac Giolla Easpaig (Place-names Section, Ordnance Survey of Ireland), Ríonach Ní Ógáin (Department of Irish Folklore, University College Dublin), Patrick Sheeran (Department of English, University College Galway) and Tim Collins (Library, University College Galway). Charles Benson (Keeper of Early Printed Books), Bernard Meehan (Keeper of Manuscripts) and their staff in Trinity College Library have been most helpful. I thank the J. M. Synge Trust and the Board of Trinity College Dublin for permission to quote from Synge's manuscripts.

A Note on the Text

The Aran Islands was first published jointly by Elkin Mathews in London and Maunsel & Co. in Dublin, in 1907. The text presented here is basically that of the first edition which does not differ substantially from Synge's corrected typescript or from the principal subsequent editions. Spelling was never Synge's strong point, as he admitted himself, but while his English was afforded the usual editorial courtesies, and the additional corrections made for this edition are too minor to be worth noting individually,* the Irish phrases scattered throughout the book have hitherto been transmitted uncorrected from edition to edition. These sacrosanct errors include three grammatical mistakes Synge certainly would have corrected had they been pointed out to him,† a running together of two words where a slight ambiguity in his typescript obviously misled a typesetter with no Irish, and the omission in perhaps fifty per cent of cases of the *síneadh fada*, the accent by which a long vowel is marked. These deficiencies have been supplied here; also, since the spelling of Irish has been simplified and standardized since Synge's day, and as his own spelling does not preserve significant dialectal or personal usages, it has been regularized for this edition. Synge's spelling of personal names, some in Irish, some in English and some in a mixture of the two that is evidently intended to give the English reader an idea of their pronunciation, led him into some awkwardnesses. For instance he calls his guide in the big island Mourteen; but this fails to represent the sound of the Irish

* Perhaps, though, I should note 'him and him' for 'him and her' (p. 36, line 30), since the change restores (Hiberno-English) sense to the passage.
† In terms of the old orthography, these are: omission of the second 'i' in *siubhail* (p. 71); omission of the 't-' in *an t-iasgaire* (p. 86); omission of the 'h' in *Bhuail* (p. 95). The omission of the particle *'an'* in the sentence on p. 78 perhaps merely reflects the casualness of speech.

Máirtín, and tricks him into trying to indicate the vocative by '*a Mhourteen*', which offends equally against English and Irish orthography. So I have thought it better to put such names into their modern Irish spelling, which is simple enough in any case. The name Michael and a few others for which Synge used the English version consistently have been left as he wrote them, as have a few words long adopted from Irish into Hiberno-English with rather variable spelling, such as curagh for the Irish *curach*, 'canoe'.

THE ARAN ISLANDS

Introduction

The geography of the Aran Islands is very simple, yet it may need a word to itself. There are three islands: Aranmor, the north island, about nine miles long; Inishmaan, the middle island, about three miles and a half across, and nearly round in form; and the south island, Inishere – in Irish, east island, – like the middle island but slightly smaller. They lie about thirty miles from Galway, up the centre of the bay, but they are not far from the cliffs of County Clare, on the south, or the corner of Connemara on the north.

Kilronan, the principal village on Aranmor, has been so much changed by the fishing industry, developed there by the Congested Districts Board,[1] that it has now very little to distinguish it from any fishing village on the west coast of Ireland. The other islands are more primitive, but even on them many changes are being made, that it was not worth while to deal with in the text.

In the pages that follow I have given a direct account of my life on the islands, and of what I met with among them, inventing nothing, and changing nothing that is essential. As far as possible, however, I have disguised the identity of the people I speak of, by making changes in their names, and in the letters I quote, and by altering some local and family relationships. I have had nothing to say about them that was not wholly in their favour, but I have made this disguise to keep them from ever feeling that a too direct use had been made of their kindness, and friendship, for which I am more grateful than it is easy to say.

PART I

I am in Aranmor, sitting over a turf fire, listening to a murmur of Gaelic that is rising from a little public-house under my room.

The steamer which comes to Aran sails according to the tide, and it was six o'clock this morning when we left the quay of Galway in a dense shroud of mist.

A low line of shore was visible at first on the right between the movement of the waves and fog, but when we came further it was lost sight of, and nothing could be seen but the mist curling in the rigging, and a small circle of foam.

There were few passengers; a couple of men going out with young pigs tied loosely in sacking, three or four young girls who sat in the cabin with their heads completely twisted in their shawls, and a builder, on his way to repair the pier at Kilronan, who walked up and down and talked with me.

In about three hours Aran came in sight. A dreary rock appeared at first sloping up from the sea into the fog; then, as we drew nearer, a coastguard station and the village.

A little later I was wandering out along the one good roadway of the island, looking over low walls on either side into small flat fields of naked rock. I have seen nothing so desolate. Grey floods of water were sweeping everywhere upon the limestone, making at times a wild torrent of the road, which twined continually over low hills and cavities in the rock or passed between a few small fields of potatoes or grass hidden away in corners that had shelter. Whenever the cloud lifted I could see the edge of the sea below me on the right, and the naked ridge of the island above me on the other side. Occasionally I passed a lonely chapel or schoolhouse, or a line of stone pillars with crosses above them and inscriptions asking a prayer for the soul of the person they commemorated.

I met few people; but here and there a band of tall girls passed me on their way to Kilronan, and called out to me with humorous wonder, speaking English with a slight foreign intonation that differed a good deal from the brogue of Galway. The rain and cold seemed to have no influence on their vitality, and as they hurried past me with eager laughter and great talking in Gaelic, they left the wet masses of rock more desolate than before.

A little after midday when I was coming back one old half-blind man spoke to me in Gaelic, but, in general, I was surprised at the abundance and fluency of the foreign tongue.

In the afternoon the rain continued, so I sat here in the inn looking out through the mist at a few men who were unlading hookers that had come in with turf from Connemara, and at the long-legged pigs that were playing in the surf. As the fishermen came in and out of the public-house underneath my room, I could hear through the broken panes that a number of them still used the Gaelic, though it seems to be falling out of use among the younger people of this village.

The old woman of the house had promised to get me a teacher of the language, and after a while I heard a shuffling on the stairs, and the old dark man I had spoken to in the morning groped his way into the room.

I brought him over to the fire, and we talked for many hours. He told me that he had known Petrie and Sir William Wilde, and many living antiquarians, and had taught Irish to Dr Finck and Dr Pedersen, and given stories to Mr Curtin of America.[2] A little after middle age he had fallen over a cliff, and since then he had had little eyesight, and a trembling of his hands and head.

As we talked he sat huddled together over the fire, shaking and blind, yet his face was indescribably pliant, lighting up with an ecstasy of humour when he told me anything that had a point of wit or malice, and growing sombre and desolate again when he spoke of religion or the fairies.

He had great confidence in his own powers and talent, and in the superiority of his stories over all other stories in the world. When we were speaking of Mr Curtin, he told me that this gentleman had brought out a volume of his Aran stories in America, and made five hundred pounds by the sale of them.

'And what do you think he did then?' he continued; 'he wrote a book of his own stories after making that lot of money with mine. And he brought them out, and the divil a halfpenny did he get for them. Would you believe that?'

Afterwards he told me how one of his children had been taken by the fairies.

One day a neighbour was passing, and she said, when she saw it on the road, 'That's a fine child.'

Its mother tried to say, 'God bless it,' but something choked the words in her throat.

A while later they found a wound on its neck, and for three nights the house was filled with noises.

'I never wear a shirt at night,' he said, 'but I got up out of my bed, all naked as I was, when I heard the noises in the house, and lighted a light, but there was nothing in it.'

Then a dummy came and made signs of hammering nails in a coffin.

The next day the seed potatoes were full of blood, and the child told his mother that he was going to America.

That night it died, and 'Believe me,' said the old man, 'the fairies were in it.'

When he went away, a little bare-footed girl was sent up with turf and the bellows to make a fire that would last for the evening.

She was shy, yet eager to talk, and told me that she had good spoken Irish, and was learning to read it in the school, and that she had been twice to Galway, though there are many grown women in the place who have never set a foot upon the mainland.

The rain has cleared off, and I have had my first real introduction to the island and its people.

I went out through Killeany – the poorest village in Aranmor – to a long neck of sandhill that runs out into the sea towards the south-west. As I lay there on the grass the clouds lifted from the Connemara mountains and, for a moment, the green undulating foreground, backed in the distance by a mass of hills, reminded me of the country near Rome. Then the dun top-sail of a hooker swept above the edge of the sandhill and revealed the presence of the sea.

As I moved on a boy and a man came down from the next village to talk to me, and I found that here, at least, English was imperfectly understood. When I asked them if there were any trees in the island they held a hurried consultation in Gaelic, and then the man asked if 'tree' meant the same thing as 'bush', for if so there were a few in sheltered hollows to the east.

They walked on with me to the sound which separates this island from Inishmaan – the middle island of the group – and showed me the roll from the Atlantic running up between two walls of cliff.

They told me that several men had stayed on Inishmaan to learn Irish, and the boy pointed out a line of hovels where they had lodged running like a belt of straw round the middle of the island. The place looked hardly fit for habitation. There was no green to be seen, and no sign of the people except these beehive-like roofs, and the outline of a Dun[3] that stood out above them against the edge of the sky.

After a while my companions went away and two other boys came and walked at my heels, till I turned and made them talk to me. They spoke at first of their poverty, and then one of them said –

'I dare say you do have to pay ten shillings a week in the hotel?'

'More,' I answered.

'Twelve?'

'More.'

'Fifteen?'

'More still.'

Then he drew back and did not question me any further, either thinking that I had lied to check his curiosity, or too awed by my riches to continue.

Repassing Killeany I was joined by a man who had spent twenty years in America, where he had lost his health and then returned, so long ago that he had forgotten English and could hardly make me understand him. He seemed hopeless, dirty, and asthmatic, and after going with me for a few hundred yards he stopped and asked for coppers. I had none left, so I gave him a fill of tobacco, and he went back to his hovel.

When he was gone, two little girls took their place behind me and I drew them in turn into conversation.

They spoke with a delicate exotic intonation that was full of charm, and told me with a sort of chant how they guide 'ladies and gintlemins' in the summer to all that is worth seeing in their neighbourhood, and sell them pampooties and maidenhair ferns, which are common among the rocks.

We were now in Kilronan, and as we parted they showed me holes in their own pampooties, or cowskin sandals, and asked me the price of new ones. I told them that my purse was empty, and then with a few quaint words of blessing they turned away from me and went down to the pier.

All this walk back had been extraordinarily fine. The intense insular clearness one sees only in Ireland, and after rain, was throwing out every ripple in the sea and sky, and every crevice in the hills beyond the bay.

This evening an old man came to see me, and said he had known a relative of mine who passed some time on this island forty-three years ago.[4]

'I was standing under the pier-wall mending nets,' he said, 'when you came off the steamer, and I said to myself in that moment, if there is a man of the name of Synge left walking the world, it is that man yonder will be he.'

He went on to complain in curiously simple yet dignified language of the changes that have taken place here since he left the island to go to sea before the end of his childhood.

'I have come back,' he said, 'to live in a bit of a house with my sister. The island is not the same at all to what it was. It is little good I can get from the people who are in it now, and anything I have to give them they don't care to have.'

From what I hear this man seems to have shut himself up in a world of individual conceits and theories, and to live aloof at his trade of net-mending, regarded by the other islanders with respect and half-ironical sympathy.

A little later when I went down to the kitchen I found two men from Inishmaan who had been benighted on the island. They seemed a simpler and perhaps a more interesting type than the people here, and talked with careful English about the history of the Duns, and the Book of Ballymote, and the Book of Kells, and other ancient MSS, with the names of which they seemed familiar.

In spite of the charm of my teacher, the old blind man I met the day of my arrival, I have decided to move on to Inishmaan, where Gaelic is more generally used, and the life is perhaps the most primitive that is left in Europe.

I spent all this last day with my blind guide, looking at the antiquities that abound in the west or north-west of the island.

As we set out I noticed among the groups of girls who smiled at our fellowship – old Máirtín says we are like the cuckoo with its pipit – a beautiful oval face with the singularly spiritual expression that is so marked in one type of the West Ireland women. Later in the day, as the old man talked continually of the fairies and the women they have taken, it seemed that there was a possible link between the wild mythology that is accepted on the islands and the strange beauty of the women.

At midday we rested near the ruins of a house, and two beautiful boys came up and sat near us. Old Máirtín asked them why the house was in ruins, and who had lived in it.

'A rich farmer built it a while since,' they said, 'but after two years he was driven away by the fairy host.'

The boys came on with us some distance to the north to visit one of the ancient beehive dwellings that is still in perfect preservation.[5] When we crawled in on our hands and knees, and stood up in the gloom of the interior, old Máirtín took a freak of earthly humour and began telling what he would have done if he could have come in there when he was a young man and a young girl along with him.

Then he sat down in the middle of the floor and began to recite old Irish poetry, with an exquisite purity of intonation that brought tears to my eyes though I understood but little of the meaning.

On our way home he gave me the Catholic theory of the fairies.

When Lucifer saw himself in the glass he thought himself equal with God. Then the Lord threw him out of Heaven, and all the angels that belonged to him. While He was 'chucking them out', an archangel asked Him to spare some of them, and those that were falling are in the air still, and have power to wreck ships, and to work evil in the world.

From this he wandered off into tedious matters of theology, and repeated many long prayers and sermons in Irish that he had heard from the priests.

A little further on we came to a slated house, and I asked him who was living in it.

'A kind of a schoolmistress,' he said; then his old face puckered with a gleam of pagan malice.

'Ah, master,' he said, 'wouldn't it be fine to be in there, and to be kissing her?'

A couple of miles from this village we turned aside to look at an old ruined church of the Ceathrar Álainn (The Four Beautiful Persons), and a holy well near it that is famous for cures of blindness and epilepsy.[6]

As we sat near the well a very old man came up from a cottage near the road, and told me how it had become famous.

'A woman of Sligo had a son who was born blind, and one night she dreamed that she saw an island with a blessed well in it that could cure her son. She told her dream in the morning, and an old man said it was of Aran she was after dreaming.

'She brought her son down by the coast of Galway, and came out in a curagh, and landed below where you see a bit of a cove.

'She walked up then to the house of my father – God rest his soul – and she told them what she was looking for.

'My father said that there was a well like what she had dreamed of, and that he would send a boy along with her to show her the way.

'"There's no need, at all," said she; "haven't I seen it all in my dream?"

'Then she went out with the child and walked up to this

well, and she kneeled down and began saying her prayers. Then she put her hand out for the water, and put it on his eyes, and the moment it touched him he called out: "O mother, look at the pretty flowers!"'

After that Máirtín described the feats of poteen[7] drinking and fighting that he did in his youth, and went on to talk of Diarmaid, who was the strongest man after Samson, and of one of the beds of Diarmaid and Gráinne, which is on the east of the island.[8] He says that Diarmaid was killed by the druids, who put a burning shirt on him, – a fragment of mythology that may connect Diarmaid with the legend of Hercules, if it is not due to the 'learning' in some hedge-school master's ballad.

Then we talked about Inishmaan.

'You'll have an old man to talk with you over there,' he said, 'and tell you stories of the fairies, but he's walking about with two sticks under him this ten year. Did ever you hear what it is goes on four legs when it is young, and on two legs after that, and on three legs when it does be old?'

I gave him the answer.

'Ah, master,' he said, 'you're a cute one, and the blessing of God be on you. Well, I'm on three legs this minute, but the old man beyond is back on four; I don't know if I'm better than the way he is; he's got his sight and I'm only an old dark man.'

I am settled at last on Inishmaan in a small cottage with a continual drone of Gaelic coming from the kitchen that opens into my room.

Early this morning the man of the house came over for me with a four-oared curagh[9] – that is, a curagh with four rowers and four oars on either side, as each man uses two – and we set off a little before noon.

It gave me a moment of exquisite satisfaction to find myself moving away from civilization in this rude canvas canoe of a model that has served primitive races since men first went on the sea.

We had to stop for a moment at a hulk[10] that is anchored in the bay, to make some arrangements for the fish-curing of the middle island, and my crew called out as soon as we were within earshot that they had a man with them who had been in France a month from this day.

When we started again, a small sail was run up in the bow, and we set off across the sound with a leaping oscillation that had no resemblance to the heavy movement of a boat.

The sail is only used as an aid, so the men continued to row after it had gone up, and as they occupied the four cross-seats I lay on the canvas at the stern and the frame of slender laths, which bent and quivered as the waves passed under them.

When we set off it was a brilliant morning of April, and the green, glittering waves seemed to toss the canoe among themselves, yet as we drew nearer this island a sudden thunderstorm broke out behind the rocks we were approaching, and lent a momentary tumult to this still vein of the Atlantic.

We landed at a small pier, from which a rude track leads up to the village between small fields and bare sheets of rock like those in Aranmor. The youngest son of my boatman, a boy of about seventeen, who is to be my teacher and guide, was waiting for me at the pier and guided me to his house, while the men settled the curagh and followed slowly with my baggage.

My room is at one end of the cottage, with a boarded floor and ceiling, and two windows opposite each other. Then there is the kitchen with earth floor and open rafters, and two doors opposite each other opening into the open air, but no windows. Beyond it there are two small rooms of half the width of the kitchen with one window apiece.

The kitchen itself, where I will spend most of my time, is full of beauty and distinction. The red dresses of the women who cluster round the fire on their stools give a glow of almost Eastern richness, and the walls have been toned by the turf-smoke to a soft brown that blends with the grey earth-colour of the floor. Many sorts of fishing-tackle, and the nets and oilskins of the men, are hung upon the walls or among the open rafters; and right overhead, under the thatch, there is a whole cowskin from which they make pampooties.[11]

Every article on these islands has an almost personal character, which gives this simple life, where all art is unknown, something of the artistic beauty of medieval life. The curaghs and spinning-wheels, the tiny wooden barrels that are still much used in the place of earthenware, the homemade cradles, churns, and baskets, are all full of individuality, and being made from materials that are common here, yet to some extent peculiar to the island, they seem to exist as a natural link between the people and the world that is about them.

The simplicity and unity of the dress increases in another way the local air of beauty. The women wear red petticoats and jackets of the island wool stained with madder, to which they usually add a plaid shawl twisted round their chests and tied at the back. When it rains they throw another petticoat over their heads with the waistband round their faces, or, if they are young, they use a heavy shawl like those worn in Galway. Occasionally other wraps are worn, and during the thunderstorm I arrived in I saw several girls with men's waistcoats buttoned round their bodies. Their skirts do not come much below the knee, and show their powerful legs in the heavy indigo stockings with which they are all provided.

The men wear three colours: the natural wool, indigo, and a grey flannel that is woven of alternate threads of indigo and the natural wool. In Aranmor many of the younger men have adopted the usual fisherman's jersey, but I have only seen one on this island.[12]

As flannel is cheap – the women spin the yarn from the wool of their own sheep, and it is then woven by a weaver in Kilronan for fourpence a yard – the men seem to wear an indefinite number of waistcoats and woollen drawers one over the other. They are usually surprised at the lightness of my own dress, and one old man I spoke to for a minute on the pier, when I came ashore, asked me if I was not cold with 'my little clothes'.

As I sat in the kitchen to dry the spray from my coat, several men who had seen me walking up came in to talk to me, usually murmuring on the threshold, 'The blessing of God on this place,' or some similar words.

The courtesy of the old woman of the house is singularly attractive, and though I could not understand much of what she said – she has no English – I could see with how much grace she motioned each visitor to a chair, or stool, according to his age, and said a few words to him till he drifted into our English conversation.

For the moment my own arrival is the chief subject of interest, and the men who come in are eager to talk to me.

Some of them express themselves more correctly than the ordinary peasant, others use the Gaelic idioms continually and substitute 'he' or 'she' for 'it', as the neuter pronoun is not found in modern Irish.

A few of the men have a curiously full vocabulary, others know only the commonest words in English, and are driven to ingenious devices to express their meaning. Of all the subjects we can talk of war seems their favourite, and the conflict between America and Spain is causing a great deal of excitement. Nearly all the families have relations who have had to cross the Atlantic, and all eat of the flour and bacon that is brought from the United States, so they have a vague fear that 'if anything happened to America', their own island would cease to be habitable.

Foreign languages are another favourite topic, and as these men are bilingual they have a fair notion of what it means to speak and think in many different idioms. Most of the strangers they see on the islands are philological students, and the people have been led to conclude that linguistic studies, particularly Gaelic studies, are the chief occupation of the outside world.

'I have seen Frenchmen, and Danes, and Germans,' said one man, 'and there does be a power of Irish books along with them, and they reading them better than ourselves. Believe me there are few rich men now in the world who are not studying the Gaelic.'

They sometimes ask me the French for simple phrases, and when they have listened to the intonation for a moment, most of them are able to reproduce it with admirable precision.

When I was going out this morning to walk round the island with Michael, the boy who is teaching me Irish, I met an old man making his way down to the cottage. He was dressed in miserable black clothes which seemed to have come from the mainland, and was so bent with rheumatism that, at a little distance, he looked more like a spider than a human being.

Michael told me it was Pat Dirane, the story-teller old Máirtín had spoken of on the other island. I wished to turn back, as he appeared to be on his way to visit me, but Michael would not hear of it.

'He will be sitting by the fire when we come in,' he said; 'let you not be afraid, there will be time enough to be talking to him by and by.'

He was right. As I came down into the kitchen some hours later old Pat was still in the chimney-corner, blinking with the turf smoke.

He spoke English with remarkable aptness and fluency, due, I believe, to the months he spent in the English provinces working at the harvest when he was a young man.

After a few formal compliments he told me how he had been crippled by an attack of the 'old hin' (i.e., the influenza), and had been complaining ever since in addition to his rheumatism.

While the old woman was cooking my dinner he asked me if I liked stories, and offered to tell one in English, though he added, it would be much better if I could follow the Gaelic. Then he began:

There were two farmers in County Clare. One had a son, and the other, a fine rich man, had a daughter.

The young man was wishing to marry the girl, and his father told him to try and get her if he thought well, though a power of gold would be wanting to get the like of her.

'I will try,' said the young man.

He put all his gold into a bag. Then he went over to the other farm, and threw in the gold in front of him.

'Is that all gold?' said the father of the girl.

'All gold,' said O'Conor (the young man's name was O'Conor).

'It will not weigh down my daughter,' said the father.

'We'll see that,' said O'Conor.

Then they put them in the scales, the daughter in one side and the gold in the other. The girl went down against the ground, so O'Conor took his bag and went out on the road.

As he was going along he came to where there was a little man, and he standing with his back against the wall.

'Where are you going with the bag?' said the little man.

'Going home,' said O'Conor.

'Is it gold you might be wanting?' said the man.

'It is, surely,' said O'Conor.

'I'll give you what you are wanting,' said the man, 'and we can bargain in this way – you'll pay me back in a year the gold I give you, or you'll pay me with five pounds cut off your own flesh.'

That bargain was made between them. The man gave a bag of gold to O'Conor, and he went back with it, and was married to the young woman.

They were rich people, and he built her a grand castle on the cliffs of Clare, with a window that looked out straightly over the wild ocean.

One day when he went up with his wife to look out over the wild ocean, he saw a ship coming in on the rocks, and no sails on her at all. She was wrecked on the rocks, and it was tea that was in her, and fine silk.

O'Conor and his wife went down to look at the wreck, and when the lady O'Conor saw the silk she said she wished a dress of it.

They got the silk from the sailors, and when the Captain came up to get the money for it, O'Conor asked him to come again and take his dinner with them. They had a grand dinner, and they drank after it, and the Captain was tipsy. While they were still drinking, a letter came to O'Conor, and it was in the letter that a friend of his was dead, and that he would have to go away on a long journey. As he was getting ready the Captain came to him.

'Are you fond of your wife?' said the Captain.

'I am fond of her,' said O'Conor.

'Will you make me a bet of twenty guineas no man comes near her while you'll be away on the journey?' said the Captain.

'I will bet it,' said O'Conor; and he went away.

There was an old hag who sold small things on the road near the castle, and the lady O'Conor allowed her to sleep up in her room in a big box. The Captain went down on the road to the old hag.

'For how much will you let me sleep one night in your box?' said the Captain.

'For no money at all would I do such a thing,' said the hag.

'For ten guineas?' said the Captain.

'Not for ten guineas,' said the hag.

'For twelve guineas?' said the Captain.

'Not for twelve guineas,' said the hag.

'For fifteen guineas?' said the Captain.

'For fifteen I will do it,' said the hag.

Then she took him up and hid him in the box. When night came the lady O'Conor walked up into her room, and the Captain watched her through a hole that was in the box. He saw her take off her two rings and put them on a kind of a board that was over her head like a chimneypiece, and take off her clothes, except her shift, and go up into her bed.

As soon as she was asleep the Captain came out of his box, and he had some means of making a light, for he lit the candle. He went over to the bed where she was sleeping without disturbing her at all, or doing any bad thing, and he took the two rings off the board, and blew out the light, and went down again into the box.

He paused for a moment, and a deep sigh of relief rose from the men and women who had crowded in while the story was going on, till the kitchen was filled with people.

As the Captain was coming out of his box the girls, who had appeared to know no English, stopped their spinning and held their breath with expectation.

The old man went on –

When O'Conor came back the Captain met him, and told him that he had been a night in his wife's room, and gave him the two rings.

O'Conor gave him the twenty guineas of the bet. Then he went up into the castle, and he took his wife up to look out of the window over the wild ocean. While she was looking he pushed her from behind, and she fell down over the cliff into the sea.

An old woman was on the shore, and she saw her falling. She went down then to the surf and pulled her out all wet and in great disorder, and she took the wet clothes off of her, and put on some old rags belonging to herself.

When O'Conor had pushed his wife from the window he went away into the land.

After a while the lady O'Conor went out searching for him, and when she had gone here and there a long time in the country, she heard that he was reaping in a field with sixty men.

She came to the field and she wanted to go in, but the gate-man would not open the gate for her. Then the owner came by, and she told him her story. He brought her in, and her husband was there, reaping, but he never gave any sign of knowing her. She showed him to the owner, and he made the man come out and go with his wife.

Then the lady O'Conor took him out on the road where there were horses, and they rode away.

When they came to the place where O'Conor had met the little man, he was there on the road before them.

'Have you my gold on you?' said the man.

'I have not,' said O'Conor.

'Then you'll pay me the flesh off your body,' said the man.

They went into a house, and a knife was brought, and a clean white cloth was put on the table, and O'Conor was put upon the cloth.

Then the little man was going to strike the lancet into him, when says lady O'Conor –

'Have you bargained for five pounds of flesh?'

'For five pounds of flesh,' said the man.

'Have you bargained for any drop of his blood?' said lady O'Conor.

'For no blood,' said the man.

'Cut out the flesh,' said lady O'Conor, 'but if you spill one drop of his blood I'll put that through you.' And she put a pistol to his head.

The little man went away and they saw no more of him.

When they got home to their castle they made a great supper, and they invited the Captain and the old hag, and the old woman that had pulled the lady O'Conor out of the sea.

After they had eaten well the lady O'Conor began, and she said they would all tell their stories. Then she told how she had been saved from the sea, and how she had found her husband.

Then the old woman told her story, the way she had found the lady O'Conor wet, and in great disorder, and had brought her in and put on her some old rags of her own.

The lady O'Conor asked the Captain for his story, but he said they would get no story from him. Then she took her pistol out of her pocket, and she put it on the edge of the table, and she said that any one that would not tell his story would get a bullet into him.

Then the Captain told the way he had got into the box, and come over to her bed without touching her at all, and had taken away the rings.

Then the lady O'Conor took the pistol and shot the hag through the body, and they threw her over the cliff into the sea.

That is my story.[13]

It gave me a strange feeling of wonder to hear this illiterate native of a wet rock in the Atlantic telling a story that is so full of European associations.

The incident of the faithful wife takes us beyond Cymbeline to the sunshine on the Arno, and the gay company who went out from Florence to tell narratives of love. It takes us again to the low vineyards of Würzburg on the Main, where the same tale was told in the middle ages, of the 'Two Merchants and the Faithful Wife of Ruprecht von Würzburg'.

The other portion, dealing with the pound of flesh, has a still wider distribution, reaching from Persia and Egypt to the

Gesta Romanorum, and the *Pecorone* of Ser Giovanni, a Florentine notary.

The present union of the two tales has already been found among the Gaels, and there is a somewhat similar version in Campbell's *Popular Tales of the Western Highlands.*

Michael walks so fast when I am out with him that I cannot pick my steps, and the sharp-edged fossils which abound in the limestone have cut my shoes to pieces.

The family held a consultation on them last night, and in the end it was decided to make me a pair of pampooties, which I have been wearing today among the rocks.

They consist simply of a piece of raw cowskin, with the hair outside, laced over the toe and round the heel with two ends of fishing-line that work round and are tied above the instep.

In the evening, when they are taken off, they are placed in a basin of water, as the rough hide cuts the foot and stocking if it is allowed to harden. For the same reason the people often step into the surf during the day, so that their feet are continually moist.

At first I threw my weight upon my heels, as one does naturally in a boot, and was a good deal bruised, but after a few hours I learned the natural walk of man, and could follow my guide in any portion of the island.

In one district below the cliffs, towards the north, one goes for nearly a mile jumping from one rock to another without a single ordinary step; and here I realized that toes have a natural use, for I found myself jumping towards any tiny crevice in the rock before me, and clinging with an eager grip in which all the muscles of my feet ached from their exertion.

The absence of the heavy boot of Europe has preserved to these people the agile walk of the wild animal, while the general simplicity of their lives has given them many other points of physical perfection. Their way of life has never been acted on by anything much more artificial than the nests and burrows of the creatures that live round them, and they seem, in a certain sense, to approach more nearly to the finer types of our aristocracies – who are bred artificially to a natural ideal – than to the labourer or citizen, as the wild horse resembles the thoroughbred rather than the hack or cart-horse. Tribes of the same natural development are, perhaps, frequent in half-civilized countries, but here a touch of the refinement of old societies is blended, with singular effect, among the qualities of the wild animal.

While I am walking with Michael some one often comes to me to ask the time of day. Few of the people, however, are sufficiently used to modern time to understand in more than a vague way the convention of the hours, and when I tell them what o'clock it is by my watch they are not satisfied, and ask how long is left them before the twilight.

The general knowledge of time on the island depends, curiously enough, on the direction of the wind. Nearly all the cottages are built, like this one, with two doors opposite each other, the more sheltered of which lies open all day to give light to the interior. If the wind is northerly the south door is opened, and the shadow of the door-post moving across the kitchen floor indicates the hour; as soon, however, as the wind changes to the south the other door is opened, and the people, who never think of putting up a primitive dial, are at a loss.

This system of doorways has another curious result. It usually happens that all the doors on one side of the village pathway are lying open with women sitting about on the thresholds, while on the other side the doors are shut and there is no sign of life. The moment the wind changes everything is reversed, and sometimes when I come back to the village after an hour's walk there seems to have been a general flight from one side of the way to the other.

In my own cottage the change of the doors alters the whole tone of the kitchen, turning it from a brilliantly-lighted room looking out on a yard and laneway to a sombre cell with a superb view of the sea.

When the wind is from the north the old woman manages my meals with fair regularity, but on the other days she often makes my tea at three o'clock instead of six. If I refuse it she puts it down to simmer for three hours in the turf, and then brings it in at six o'clock full of anxiety to know if it is warm enough.

The old man is suggesting that I should send him a clock when I go away. He'd like to have something from me in the house, he says, the way they wouldn't forget me, and wouldn't a clock be as handy as another thing, and they'd be thinking on me whenever they'd look on its face.

The general ignorance of any precise hours in the day makes it impossible for the people to have regular meals.

They seem to eat together in the evening, and sometimes in the morning, a little after dawn, before they scatter for their work, but during the day they simply drink a cup of tea and eat a piece of bread, or some potatoes, whenever they are hungry.

For men who live in the open air they eat strangely little. Often when Michael has been out weeding potatoes for eight or nine hours without food, he comes in and eats a few slices of home-made bread, and then he is ready to go out with me and wander for hours about the island.

They use no animal food except a little bacon and salt fish. The old woman says she would be very ill if she ate fresh meat.

Some years ago, before tea, sugar, and flour had come into general use, salt fish was much more the staple article of diet than at present, and, I am told, skin diseases were very common, though they are now rare on the islands.

No one who has not lived for weeks among these grey clouds and seas can realize the joy with which the eye rests on the red dresses of the women, especially when a number of them are to be found together, as happened early this morning.

I heard that the young cattle were to be shipped for a fair on the mainland, which is to take place in a few days, and I went down on the pier, a little after dawn, to watch them.

The bay was shrouded in the greys of coming rain, yet the thinness of the cloud threw a silvery light on the sea, and an unusual depth of blue to the mountains of Connemara.

As I was going across the sandhills one dun-sailed hooker[14] glided slowly out to begin her voyage, and another beat up to the pier. Troops of red cattle, driven mostly by the women, were coming up from several directions, forming, with the green of the long tract of grass that separates the sea from the rocks, a new unity of colour.

The pier itself was crowded with bullocks and a great number of the people. I noticed one extraordinary girl in the throng who seemed to exert an authority on all who came near her. Her curiously-formed nostrils and narrow chin gave her a witch-like expression, yet the beauty of her hair and skin made her singularly attractive.

When the empty hooker was made fast its deck was still many feet below the level of the pier, so the animals were slung down by a rope from the mast-head, with much struggling and confusion. Some of them made wild efforts to escape, nearly carrying their owners with them into the sea, but they were handled with wonderful dexterity, and there was no mishap.

When the open hold was filled with young cattle, packed as tightly as they could stand, the owners with their wives or sisters, who go with them to prevent extravagance in Galway, jumped down on the deck, and the voyage was begun. Immediately afterwards a rickety old hooker beat up with turf from Connemara,[15] and while she was unlading all the men sat along the edge of the pier and made remarks upon the rottenness of her timber till the owners grew wild with rage.

The tide was now too low for more boats to come to the pier, so a move was made to a strip of sand towards the southeast, where the rest of the cattle were shipped through the surf. Here the hooker was anchored about eighty yards from the shore, and a curagh was rowed round to tow out the animals. Each bullock was caught in its turn and girded with a sling of rope by which it could be hoisted on board. Another rope was fastened to the horns and passed out to a man in the stern of the curagh. Then the animal was forced down through the surf and out of its depth before it had much time to struggle. Once fairly swimming, it was towed out to the hooker and dragged on board in a half-drowned condition.

The freedom of the sand seemed to give a stronger spirit of revolt, and some of the animals were only caught after a dangerous struggle. The first attempt was not always successful, and

I saw one three-year-old lift two men with his horns, and drag another fifty yards along the sand by his tail before he was subdued.

While this work was going on a crowd of girls and women collected on the edge of the cliff and kept shouting down a confused babble of satire and praise.

When I came back to the cottage I found that among the women who had gone to the mainland was a daughter of the old woman's, and that her baby of about nine months had been left in the care of its grandmother.

As I came in she was busy getting ready my dinner, and old Pat Dirane, who usually comes at this hour, was rocking the cradle. It is made of clumsy wicker-work, with two pieces of rough wood fastened underneath to serve as rockers, and all the time I am in my room I can hear it bumping on the floor with extraordinary violence. When the baby is awake it sprawls on the floor, and the old woman sings it a variety of inarticulate lullabies that have much musical charm.

Another daughter, who lives at home, has gone to the fair also, so the old woman has both the baby and myself to take care of as well as a crowd of chickens that live in a hole beside the fire. Often when I want tea, or when the old woman goes for water, I have to take my own turn at rocking the cradle.

One of the largest Duns,[16] or pagan forts, on the islands, is within a stone's-throw of my cottage, and I often stroll up there after a dinner of eggs or salt pork, to smoke drowsily on the stones. The neighbours know my habit, and not infrequently some one wanders up to ask what news there is in the last paper I have received, or to make inquiries about the American war. If no one comes I prop my book open with stones touched by the Fir-bolgs,[17] and sleep for hours in the delicious warmth of the sun. The last few days I have almost lived on the round walls, for, by some miscalculation, our turf has come to an end, and the fires are kept up with dried cow-dung – a common fuel on the island – the smoke from which filters through into my room and lies in blue layers above my table and bed.

Fortunately the weather is fine, and I can spend my days in the sunshine. When I look round from the top of these walls I can see the sea on nearly every side, stretching away to distant ranges of mountains on the north and south. Underneath me to the east there is the one inhabited district of the island, where I can see red figures moving about the cottages, sending up an occasional fragment of conversation or of the old island melodies.

The baby is teething, and has been crying for several days. Since his mother went to the fair they have been feeding him with cow's milk, often slightly sour, and giving him, I think, more than he requires.

This morning, however, he seemed so unwell they sent out to look for a foster-mother in the village, and before long a young woman, who lives a little way to the east, came in and restored him his natural food.

A few hours later, when I came into the kitchen to talk to old Pat, another woman performed the same kindly office, this time a person with a curiously whimsical expression.

Pat told me a story of an unfaithful wife, which I will give further down, and then broke into a moral dispute with the visitor, which caused immense delight to some young men who had come down to listen to the story. Unfortunately it was carried on so rapidly in Gaelic that I lost most of the points.

This old man talks usually in a mournful tone about his ill-health, and his death, which he feels to be approaching, yet he has occasional touches of humour that remind me of old Máirtín on the north island. Today a grotesque twopenny doll was lying on the floor near the old woman. He picked it up and examined it as if comparing it with her. Then he held it up: 'Is it you is after bringing that thing into the world,' he said, 'woman of the house?'

Here is his story:

One day I was travelling on foot from Galway to Dublin, and the darkness came on me and I ten miles from the town I was wanting to pass the night in. Then a hard rain began to fall and I was tired walking, so when I saw a sort of a house with no roof on it up against the road, I got in the way the walls would give me shelter.

As I was looking round I saw a light in some trees two perches off, and thinking any sort of a house would be better than where I was, I got over the wall and went up to the house to look in at the window.

I saw a dead man laid on a table, and candles lighted, and a woman watching him. I was frightened when I saw him, but it was raining hard, and I said to myself, if he was dead he couldn't hurt me. Then I knocked on the door and the woman came and opened it.

'Good evening, ma'am,' says I.

'Good evening kindly, stranger,' says she. 'Come in out of the rain.'

Then she took me in and told me her husband was after dying on her, and she was watching him that night.

'But it's thirsty you'll be, stranger,' says she. 'Come into the parlour.'

Then she took me into the parlour – and it was a fine clean house – and she put a cup, with a saucer under it, on the table before me with fine sugar and bread.

When I'd had a cup of tea I went back into the kitchen where the dead man was lying, and she gave me a fine new pipe off the table with a drop of spirits.

'Stranger,' says she, 'would you be afeard to be alone with himself?'

'Not a bit in the world, ma'am,' says I; 'he that's dead can do no hurt.'

Then she said she wanted to go over and tell the neighbours the way her husband was after dying on her, and she went out and locked the door behind her.

I smoked one pipe, and I leaned out and took another off the table. I was smoking it with my hand on the back of my chair – the way you are yourself this minute, God bless you – and I looking on the dead man, when he opened his eyes as wide as myself and looked at me.

'Don't be afeard, stranger,' said the dead man; 'I'm not dead at all in the world. Come here and help me up and I'll tell you all about it.'

Well, I went up and took the sheet off of him, and I saw that he had a fine clean shirt on his body, and fine flannel drawers.

He sat up then, and says he –

'I've got a bad wife, stranger, and I let on to be dead the way I'd catch her goings on.'

Then he got two fine sticks he had to keep down his wife, and he put them at each side of his body, and he laid himself out again as if he was dead.

In half an hour his wife came back and a young man along with her. Well, she gave him his tea, and she told him he was tired, and he would do right to go and lie down in the bed-room.

The young man went in and the woman sat down to watch by the dead man. A while after she got up and 'Stranger,' says she, 'I'm going in to get the candle out of the room; I'm thinking the young man will be asleep by this time.' She went into the bedroom, but the divil a bit of her came back.

Then the dead man got up, and he took one stick, and he gave the other to myself. We went in and we saw them lying together with her head on his arm.

The dead man hit him a blow with the stick so that the blood out of him leapt up and hit the gallery.

That is my story.[18]

In stories of this kind he always speaks in the first person, with minute details to show that he was actually present at the scenes that are described.

At the beginning of this story he gave me a long account of what had made him be on his way to Dublin on that occasion, and told me about all the rich people he was going to see in the finest streets of the city.

A week of sweeping fogs has passed over and given me a strange sense of exile and desolation. I walk round the island nearly every day, yet I can see nothing anywhere but a mass of wet rock, a strip of surf, and then a tumult of waves.

The slaty limestone has grown black with the water that is dripping on it, and wherever I turn there is the same grey obsession twining and wreathing itself among the narrow fields, and the same wail from the wind that shrieks and whistles in the loose rubble of the walls.

At first the people do not give much attention to the wilderness that is round them, but after a few days their voices sink in the kitchen, and their endless talk of pigs and cattle falls to the whisper of men who are telling stories in a haunted house.

The rain continues; but this evening a number of young men were in the kitchen mending nets, and the bottle of poteen was drawn from its hiding-place.

One cannot think of these people drinking wine on the summit of this crumbling precipice, but their grey poteen, which brings a shock of joy to the blood, seems predestined to keep sanity in men who live forgotten in these worlds of mist.

I sat in the kitchen part of the evening to feel the gaiety that was rising, and when I came into my own room after dark, one of the sons came in every time the bottle made its round, to pour me out my share.

It has cleared, and the sun is shining with a luminous warmth that makes the whole island glisten with the splendour of a gem, and fills the sea and sky with a radiance of blue light.

I have come out to lie on the rocks where I have the black edge of the north island in front of me, Galway Bay, too blue almost to look at, on my right, the Atlantic on my left, a perpendicular cliff under my ankles, and over me innumerable gulls that chase each other in a white cirrus of wings.

A nest of hooded crows is somewhere near me, and one of the old birds is trying to drive me away by letting itself fall like a stone every few moments, from about forty yards above me to within reach of my hand.

Gannets are passing up and down above the sound, swooping at times after a mackerel, and further off I can see the whole fleet of hookers coming out from Kilronan for a night's fishing in the deep water to the west.

As I lie here hour after hour, I seem to enter into the wild pastimes of the cliff, and to become a companion of the cormorants and crows.

Many of the birds display themselves before me with the vanity of barbarians, performing in strange evolutions as long as I am in sight, and returning to their ledge of rock when I am gone. Some are wonderfully expert, and cut graceful figures for an inconceivable time without a flap of their wings, growing so absorbed in their own dexterity that they often collide with one another in their flight, an incident always followed by a wild outburst of abuse. Their language is easier than Gaelic, and I seem to understand the greater part of their cries, though I am not able to answer. There is one plaintive note which they take up in the middle of their usual babble with extraordinary effect, and pass on from one to another along the cliff with a sort of an inarticulate wail, as if they remembered for an instant the horror of the mist.

On the low sheets of rock to the east I can see a number of red and grey figures hurrying about their work. The continual passing in this island between the misery of last night and the splendour of today, seems to create an affinity between the moods of these people and the moods of varying rapture and dismay that are frequent in artists, and in certain forms of alienation. Yet it is only in the intonation of a few sentences or some old fragment of melody that I catch the real spirit of the island, for in general the men sit together and talk with endless iteration of the tides and fish, and of the price of kelp in Connemara.

After Mass this morning an old woman was buried. She lived in the cottage next mine, and more than once before noon I heard a faint echo of the keen. I did not go to the wake for fear my presence might jar upon the mourners, but all last evening I could hear the strokes of a hammer in the yard, where, in the middle of a little crowd of idlers, the next of kin laboured slowly at the coffin. Today, before the hour for the funeral, poteen was served to a number of men who stood about upon the road, and a portion was brought to me in my room. Then the coffin was carried out sewn loosely in sailcloth, and held near the ground by three cross-poles lashed upon the top. As we moved down to the low eastern portion of the island, nearly all the men, and all the oldest women, wearing petticoats over their heads, came out and joined in the procession.

While the grave was being opened the women sat down among the flat tombstones, bordered with a pale fringe of early bracken, and began the wild keen, or crying for the dead. Each old woman, as she took her turn in the leading recitative, seemed possessed for the moment with a profound ecstasy of grief, swaying to and fro, and bending her forehead to the stone before her, while she called out to the dead with a perpetually recurring chant of sobs.

All round the graveyard other wrinkled women, looking out from under the deep red petticoats that cloaked them, rocked themselves with the same rhythm, and intoned the inarticulate chant that is sustained by all as an accompaniment.

The morning had been beautifully fine, but as they lowered the coffin into the grave, thunder rumbled overhead and hailstones hissed among the bracken.

In Inishmaan one is forced to believe in a sympathy between man and nature, and at this moment when the thunder sounded a death-peal of extraordinary grandeur above the voices of the women, I could see the faces near me stiff and drawn with emotion.

When the coffin was in the grave, and the thunder had rolled away across the hills of Clare, the keen broke out again more passionately than before.

This grief of the keen is no personal complaint for the death of one woman over eighty years, but seems to contain the whole passionate rage that lurks somewhere in every native of the island. In this cry of pain the inner consciousness of the people seems to lay itself bare for an instant, and to reveal the mood of beings who feel their isolation in the face of a universe that wars on them with winds and seas. They are usually silent, but in the presence of death all outward show of indifference or patience is forgotten, and they shriek with pitiable despair before the horror of the fate to which they all are doomed.

Before they covered the coffin an old man kneeled down by the grave and repeated a simple prayer for the dead.

There was an irony in these words of atonement and Catholic belief spoken by voices that were still hoarse with the cries of pagan desperation.

A little beyond the grave I saw a line of old women who had recited in the keen sitting in the shadow of a wall beside the roofless shell of the church. They were still sobbing and shaken with grief, yet they were beginning to talk again of the daily trifles that veil from them the terror of the world.

When we had all come out of the graveyard, and two men had rebuilt the hole in the wall through which the coffin had been carried in, we walked back to the village, talking of anything, and joking of anything, as if merely coming from the boat-slip, or the pier.

One man told me of the poteen drinking that takes place at some funerals.

'A while since,' he said, 'there were two men fell down in the graveyard while the drink was on them. The sea was rough that day, the way no one could go to bring the doctor, and one of the men never woke again, and found death that night.'[19]

The other day the men of this house made a new field. There was a slight bank of earth under the wall of the yard, and another in the corner of the cabbage garden. The old man and his eldest son dug out the clay, with the care of men working in a gold-mine, and Michael packed it in panniers – there are no wheeled vehicles on this island – for transport to a flat rock in a sheltered corner of their holding, where it was mixed with sand and seaweed and spread out in a layer upon the stone.

Most of the potato-growing of the island is carried on in fields of this sort – for which the people pay a considerable rent – and if the season is at all dry, their hope of a fair crop is nearly always disappointed.

It is now nine days since rain has fallen, and the people are filled with anxiety, although the sun has not yet been hot enough to do harm.

The drought is also causing a scarcity of water. There are a few springs on this side of the island, but they come only from a little distance, and in hot weather are not to be relied on. The supply for this house is carried up in a water-barrel by one of the women. If it is drawn off at once it is not very nauseous, but if it has lain, as it often does, for some hours in the barrel, the smell, colour, and taste are unendurable. The water for washing is also coming short, and as I walk round the edges of the sea, I often come on a girl with her petticoats tucked up round her, standing in a pool left by the tide and washing her flannels among the sea-anemones and crabs. Their red bodices and white tapering legs make them as beautiful as tropical sea-birds, as they stand in a frame of seaweeds against the brink of the Atlantic. Michael, however, is a little uneasy when they are in sight, and I cannot pause to watch them. This habit of using the sea water for washing causes a good deal of rheumatism on the island, for the salt lies in the clothes and keeps them continually moist.

The people have taken advantage of this dry moment to begin the burning of the kelp,[20] and all the islands are lying in a volume of grey smoke. There will not be a very large quantity this year, as the people are discouraged by the uncertainty of the market, and do not care to undertake the task of manufacture without a certainty of profit.

The work needed to form a ton of kelp is considerable. The seaweed is collected from the rocks after the storms of autumn and winter, dried on fine days, and then made up into a rick, where it is left till the beginning of June.

It is then burnt in low kilns on the shore, an affair that takes from twelve to twenty-four hours of continuous hard work, though I understand the people here do not manage well and spoil a portion of what they produce by burning it more than is required.

The kiln holds about two tons of molten kelp, and when full it is loosely covered with stones, and left to cool. In a few days the substance is as hard as the limestone, and has to be broken with crowbars before it can be placed in curaghs for transport to Kilronan, where it is tested to determine the amount of iodine it contains, and paid for accordingly. In former years good kelp would bring seven pounds a ton, now four pounds are not always reached.

In Aran even manufacture is of interest. The low flame-edged kiln, sending out dense clouds of creamy smoke, with a band of red and grey clothed workers moving in the haze, and usually some petticoated boys and women who come down with drink, forms a scene with as much variety and colour as any picture from the East.

The men feel in a certain sense the distinction of their island, and show me their work with pride. One of them said to me yesterday, 'I'm thinking you never saw the like of this work before this day?'

'That is true,' I answered, 'I never did.'

'Bedad, then,' he said, 'isn't it a great wonder that you've seen France, and Germany, and the Holy Father, and never seen a man making kelp till you come to Inishmaan.'

All the horses from this island are put out on grass among the hills of Connemara from June to the end of September, as there is no grazing here during the summer.

Their shipping and transport is even more difficult than that of the horned cattle. Most of them are wild Connemara ponies, and their great strength and timidity make them hard to handle on the narrow pier, while in the hooker itself it is not easy to get them safely on their feet in the small space that is available. They are dealt with in the same way as for the bullocks I have spoken of already, but the excitement becomes much more intense, and the storm of Gaelic that rises the moment a horse is shoved from the pier, till it is safely in its place, is indescribable. Twenty boys and men howl and scream with agitation, cursing and exhorting, without knowing, most of the time, what they are saying.

Apart, however, from this primitive babble, the dexterity and power of the men are displayed to more advantage than in anything I have seen hitherto. I noticed particularly the owner of a hooker from the north island that was loaded this morning. He seemed able to hold up a horse by his single weight when it was swinging from the masthead, and preserved a humorous calm even in moments of the wildest excitement. Sometimes a large mare would come down sideways on the backs of the other horses, and kick there till the hold seemed to be filled with a mass of struggling centaurs, for the men themselves often leap down to try and save the foals from injury. The backs of the horses put in first are often a good deal cut by the shoes of the others that arrive on top of them, but otherwise they do not seem to be much the worse, and as they are not on their way to a fair, it is not of much consequence in what condition they come to land.

There is only one bit and saddle in the island, which are used by the priest, who rides from the chapel to the pier when he has held the service on Sunday.

The islanders themselves ride with a simple halter and a stick, yet sometimes travel, at least in the larger island, at a desperate gallop. As the horses usually have panniers, the rider sits sideways over the withers, and if the panniers are empty they go at full speed in this position without anything to hold to.

More than once in Aranmor I met a party going out west with empty panniers from Kilronan. Long before they came in sight I could hear a clatter of hoofs, and then a whirl of horses would come round a corner at full gallop with their heads out, utterly indifferent to the slender halter that is their only check. They generally travel in single file with a few yards between them, and as there is no traffic there is little fear of an accident.

Sometimes a woman and a man ride together, but in this case the man sits in the usual position, and the woman sits sideways behind him, and holds him round the waist.

Old Pat Dirane continues to come up every day to talk to me, and at times I turn the conversation to his experiences of the fairies.

He has seen a good many of them, he says, in different parts of the island, especially in the sandy districts north of the slip. They are about a yard high with caps like the 'peelers' pulled down over their faces. On one occasion he saw them playing ball in the evening just above the slip, and he says I must avoid that place in the morning or after nightfall for fear they might do me mischief.

He has seen two women who were 'away' with them, one a young married woman, the other a girl. The woman was standing by a wall, at a spot he described to me with great care, looking out towards the north.

Another night he heard a voice crying out in Irish, 'A mháthair, tá mé marbh' ('O mother, I'm killed'), and in the morning there was blood on the wall of his house, and a child in a house not far off was dead.

Yesterday he took me aside, and said he would tell me a secret he had never yet told to any person in the world.

'Take a sharp needle,' he said, 'and stick it in under the collar of your coat, and not one of them will be able to have power on you.'

Iron is a common talisman with barbarians, but in this case the idea of exquisite sharpness was probably present also, and, perhaps, some feeling for the sanctity of the instrument of toil, a folk-belief that is common in Brittany.

The fairies are more numerous in Mayo than in any other county, though they are fond of certain districts in Galway, where the following story is said to have taken place.

'A farmer was in great distress as his crops had failed, and his cow had died on him. One night he told his wife to make him a fine new sack for flour before the next morning; and when it was finished he started off with it before the dawn.

'At that time there was a gentleman who had been taken by the fairies, and made an officer among them, and it was often people would see him and him riding on a white horse at dawn and in the evening.

'The poor man went down to the place where they used to see the officer, and when he came by on his horse, he asked the loan of two hundred and a half of flour, for he was in great want.

'The officer called the fairies out of a hole in the rocks where they stored their wheat, and told them to give the poor man what he was asking. Then he told him to come back and pay him in a year, and rode away.

'When the poor man got home he wrote down the day on a piece of paper, and that day year he came back and paid the officer.'

When he had ended his story the old man told me that the fairies have a tenth of all the produce of the country, and make stores of it in the rocks.

It is a Holy Day, and I have come up to sit on the Dun while the people are at Mass.

A strange tranquillity has come over the island this morning, as happens sometimes on Sunday, filling the two circles of sea and sky with the quiet of a church.

The one landscape that is here lends itself with singular power to this suggestion of grey luminous cloud. There is no wind, and no definite light. Aranmor seems to sleep upon a mirror, and the hills of Connemara look so near that I am troubled by the width of the bay that lies before them, touched this morning with individual expression one sees sometimes in a lake.

On these rocks, where there is no growth of vegetable or animal life, all the seasons are the same, and this June day is so full of autumn that I listen unconsciously for the rustle of dead leaves.

The first group of men are coming out of the chapel, followed by a crowd of women, who divide at the gate and troop off in different directions, while the men linger on the road to gossip.

The silence is broken; I can hear far off, as if over water, a faint murmur of Gaelic.

In the afternoon the sun came out and I was rowed over for a visit to Kilronan.

As my men were bringing round the curagh to take me off a headland near the pier, they struck a sunken rock, and came ashore shipping a quantity of water. They plugged the hole with a piece of sacking torn from a bag of potatoes they were taking over for the priest, and we set off with nothing but a piece of torn canvas between us and the Atlantic.

Every few hundred yards one of the rowers had to stop and bail, but the hole did not increase.

When we were about half way across the sound we met a curagh coming towards us with its sail set. After some shouting in Gaelic, I learned that they had a packet of letters and tobacco for myself. We sidled up as near as was possible with the roll, and my goods were thrown to me wet with spray.

After my weeks in Inishmaan, Kilronan seemed an imposing centre of activity. The half-civilized fishermen of the larger island are inclined to despise the simplicity of the life here, and some of them who were standing about when I landed asked me how at all I passed my time with no decent fishing to be looking at.

I turned in for a moment to talk to the old couple in the hotel, and then moved on to pay some other visits in the village.

Later in the evening I walked out along the northern road, where I met many of the natives of the outlying villages, who had come down to Kilronan for the Holy Day, and were now wandering home in scattered groups.

The women and girls, when they had no men with them, usually tried to make fun with me.

'Is it tired you are, stranger?' said one girl. I was walking very slowly, to pass the time before my return to the east.

'Bedad, it is not, little girl,' I answered in Gaelic, 'it is lonely I am.'

'Here is my little sister, stranger, who will give you her arm.'

And so it went on. Quiet as these women are on ordinary occasions, when two or three of them are gathered together in their holiday petticoats and shawls, they are as wild and capricious as the women who live in towns.

About seven o'clock I got back to Kilronan, and beat up my crew from the public-houses near the bay. With their usual carelessness they had not seen to the leak in the curagh, nor to an oar that was losing the brace that holds it to the thole-pin, and we moved off across the sound at an absurd pace with a deepening pool at our feet.

A superb evening light was lying over the island, which made me rejoice at our delay. Looking back there was a golden haze behind the sharp edges of the rock, and a long wake from the sun, which was making jewels of the bubbling left by the oars.

The men had had their share of porter and were unusually voluble, pointing out things to me that I had already seen, and stopping now and then to make me notice the oily smell of mackerel that was rising from the waves.

They told me that an evicting party is coming to the island tomorrow morning, and gave me a long account of what they make and spend in the year, and of their trouble with the rent.

'The rent is hard enough for a poor man,' said one of them, 'but this time we didn't pay, and they're after serving processes on every one of us. A man will have to pay his rent now, and a power of money with it for the process, and I'm thinking the agent will have money enough out of them processes to pay for his servant-girl and his man all the year.'

I asked afterwards who the island belonged to.

'Bedad,' they said, 'we've always heard it belonged to Miss —, and she is dead.'[21]

When the sun passed like a lozenge of gold flame into the sea the cold became intense. Then the men began to talk among themselves, and losing the thread, I lay half in a dream looking at the pale oily sea about us, and the low cliffs of the island sloping up past the village with its wreath of smoke to the outline of Dun Conor.

Old Pat was in the house when I arrived, and he told a long story after supper:

There was once a widow living among the woods, and her only son living along with her. He went out every morning through the trees to get sticks, and one day as he was lying on the ground he saw a swarm of flies flying over what the cow leaves behind her. He took up his sickle and hit one blow at them, and hit that hard he left no single one of them living.

That evening he said to his mother that it was time he was going out into the world to seek his fortune, for he was able to destroy a whole swarm of flies at one blow, and he asked her to make him three cakes the way he might take them with him in the morning.

He started the next day a while after the dawn, with his three cakes in his wallet, and he ate one of them near ten o'clock.

He got hungry again by midday and ate the second, and when night was coming on him he ate the third. After that he met a man on the road who asked him where he was going.

'I'm looking for some place where I can work for my living,' said the young man.

'Come with me,' said the other man, 'and sleep tonight in the barn, and I'll give you work tomorrow to see what you're able for.'

The next morning the farmer brought him out and showed him his cows and told him to take them out to graze on the hills, and to keep good watch that no one should come near them to milk them. The young man drove out the cows into the fields, and when the heat of the day came on he lay down on his back and looked up into the sky. A while after he saw a black spot in the north-west, and it grew larger and nearer till he saw a great giant coming towards him.

He got up on to his feet and he caught the giant round the legs with his two arms, and he drove him down into the hard ground above his ankles, the way he was not able to free himself. Then the giant told him to do him no hurt, and gave him his magic rod, and told him to strike on the rock, and he would find his beautiful black horse, and his sword, and his fine suit.

The young man struck the rock and it opened before him, and he found the beautiful black horse, and the giant's sword and the suit lying before him. He took out the sword alone, and he struck one blow with it and struck off the giant's head. Then he put back the sword into the rock, and went out again to his cattle, till it was time to drive them home to the farmer.

When they came to milk the cows they found a power of milk in them, and the farmer asked the young man if he had seen nothing out on the hills, for the other cow-boys had been bringing home the cows with no drop of milk in them. And the young man said he had seen nothing.

The next day he went out again with the cows. He lay down on his back in the heat of the day, and after a while he saw a black spot in the north-west, and it grew larger and nearer, till he saw it was a great giant coming to attack him.

'You killed my brother,' said the giant; 'come here, till I make a garter of your body.'

The young man went to him and caught him by the legs and drove him into the hard ground up to his ankles.

Then he hit the rod against the rock, and took out the sword and struck off the giant's head.

That evening the farmer found twice as much milk in the cows as the evening before, and he asked the young man if he had seen anything. The young man said that he had seen nothing.

The third day the third giant came to him and said, 'You have killed my two brothers; come here, till I make a garter of your body.'

And he did with this giant as he had done with the other two, and that evening there was so much milk in the cows it was dropping out of their udders on the pathway.

The next day the farmer called him and told him he might leave the cows in the stalls that day, for there was a great curiosity to be seen, namely, a beautiful king's daughter that was to be eaten by a great fish, if there was no one in it that could save her. But the young man said such a sight was all one to him, and he went out with the cows on to the hills. When he came to the rocks he hit them with his rod and brought out the suit and put it on him, and brought out the sword and strapped it on his side, like an officer, and he got on the black horse and rode faster than the wind till he came to where the beautiful king's daughter was sitting on the shore in a golden chair, waiting for the great fish.

When the great fish came in on the sea, bigger than a whale, with two wings on the back of it, the young man went down into the surf and struck at it with his sword and cut off one of its wings. All the sea turned red with the bleeding out of it, till it swam away and left the young man on the shore.

Then he turned his horse and rode faster than the wind till

he came to the rocks, and he took the suit off him and put it back in the rocks, with the giant's sword and the black horse, and drove the cows down to the farm.

The man came out before him and said he had missed the greatest wonder ever was seen, and that a noble person was after coming down with a fine suit on him and cutting off one of the wings from the great fish.

'And there'll be the same necessity on her for two mornings more,' said the farmer, 'and you'd do right to come and look on it.'

But the young man said he would not come.

The next morning he went out with his cows, and he took the sword and the suit and the black horse out of the rock, and he rode faster than the wind till he came where the king's daughter was sitting on the shore. When the people saw him coming there was great wonder on them to know if it was the same man they had seen the day before. The king's daughter called out to him to come and kneel before her, and when he kneeled down she took her scissors and cut off a lock of hair from the back of his head and hid it in her clothes.

Then the great worm came in from the sea, and he went down into the surf and cut the other wing off from it. All the sea turned red with the bleeding out of it, till it swam away and left them.

That evening the farmer came out before him and told him of the great wonder he had missed, and asked him would he go the next day and look on it. The young man said he would not go.

The third day he came again on the black horse to where the king's daughter was sitting on a golden chair waiting for the great worm. When it came in from the sea the young man went down before it, and every time it opened its mouth to eat him, he struck into its mouth, till his sword went out through its neck, and it rolled back and died.

Then he rode off faster than the wind, and he put the suit and the sword and the black horse into the rock, and drove home the cows.

The farmer was there before him, and he told him that there

was to be a great marriage feast held for three days, and on the third day the king's daughter would be married to the man that killed the great worm, if they were able to find him.

A great feast was held, and men of great strength came and said it was themselves were after killing the great worm.

But on the third day the young man put on the suit, and strapped the sword to his side like an officer, and got on the black horse and rode faster than the wind, till he came to the palace.

The king's daughter saw him, and she brought him in and made him kneel down before her. Then she looked at the back of his head and she saw the place where she had cut off the lock with her own hand. She led him in to the king, and they were married, and the young man was given all the estate.

That is my story.[22]

Two recent attempts to carry out evictions on the island came to nothing, for each time a sudden storm rose, by, it is said, the power of a native witch, when the steamer was approaching, and made it impossible to land.[23]

This morning, however, broke beneath a clear sky of June, and when I came into the open air the sea and rocks were shining with wonderful brilliancy. Groups of men, dressed in their holiday clothes, were standing about, talking with anger and fear, yet showing a lurking satisfaction at the thought of the dramatic pageant that was to break the silence of the seas.

About half-past nine the steamer came in sight, on the narrow line of sea-horizon that is seen in the centre of the bay, and immediately a last effort was made to hide the cows and sheep of the families that were most in debt.

Till this year no one on the island would consent to act as bailiff, so that it was impossible to identify the cattle of the defaulters. Now, however, a man of the name of Patrick has sold his honour, and the effort of concealment is practically futile.

This falling away from the ancient loyalty of the island has caused intense indignation, and early yesterday morning, while I was dreaming on the Dun, this letter was nailed on the doorpost of the chapel:

'Patrick, the devil, a revolver is waiting for you. If you are missed with the first shot, there will be five more that will hit you.

'Any man that will talk with you, or work with you, or drink a pint of porter in your shop, will be done with the same way as yourself.'

As the steamer drew near I moved down with the men to watch the arrival, though no one went further than about a mile from the shore.

Two curaghs from Kilronan with a man who was to give help in identifying the cottages, the doctor, and the relieving officer, were drifting with the tide, unwilling to come to land without the support of the larger party. When the anchor had been thrown it gave me a strange throb of pain to see the boats being lowered, and the sunshine gleaming on the rifles and helmets of the constabulary who crowded into them.

Once on shore the men were formed in close marching order, a word was given, and the heavy rhythm of their boots came up over the rocks. We were collected in two straggling bands on either side of the roadway, and a few moments later the body of magnificent armed men passed close to us, followed by a low rabble, who had been brought to act as drivers for the sheriff.

After my weeks spent among primitive men this glimpse of the newer types of humanity was not reassuring. Yet these mechanical police, with the commonplace agents and sheriffs, and the rabble they had hired, represented aptly enough the civilization for which the homes of the island were to be desecrated.

A stop was made at one of the first cottages in the village, and the day's work began. Here, however, and at the next cottage, a compromise was made, as some relatives came up at the last moment and lent the money that was needed to gain a respite.

In another case a girl was ill in the house, so the doctor interposed, and the people were allowed to remain after a merely formal eviction. About midday, however, a house was reached where there was no pretext for mercy, and no money could be procured. At a sign from the sheriff the work of carrying out the beds and utensils was begun in the middle of a crowd of natives who looked on in absolute silence, broken only by the wild imprecations of the woman of the house. She belonged to one of the most primitive families on the island, and she shook with uncontrollable fury as she saw the strange armed men who spoke a language she could not understand driving her from the hearth she had brooded on for thirty years. For these people the outrage to the hearth is the supreme catastrophe. They live here in a world of grey, where there are wild rains and mists every week in the year, and their warm chimney corners, filled with children and young girls, grow into the consciousness of each family in a way it is not easy to understand in more civilized places.

The outrage to a tomb in China probably gives no greater shock to the Chinese than the outrage to a hearth in Inishmaan gives to the people.

When the few trifles had been carried out, and the door blocked with stones, the old woman sat down by the threshold and covered her head with her shawl.

Five or six other women who lived close by sat down in a circle round her, with mute sympathy. Then the crowd moved on with the police to another cottage where the same scene was to take place, and left the group of desolate women sitting by the hovel.

There were still no clouds in the sky, and the heat was intense. The police when not in motion lay sweating and gasping under the walls with their tunics unbuttoned. They were not attractive, and I kept comparing them with the islandmen, who walked up and down as cool and fresh-looking as the sea-gulls.

When the last eviction had been carried out a division was made: half the party went off with the bailiff to search the inner plain of the island for the cattle that had been hidden in the morning, the other half remained on the village road to guard some pigs that had already been taken possession of.

After a while two of these pigs escaped from the drivers and began a wild race up and down the narrow road. The people shrieked and howled to increase their terror, and at last some of them became so excited that the police thought it time to interfere. They drew up in double line opposite the mouth of a blind laneway where the animals had been shut up. A moment later the shrieking began again in the west and the two pigs came in sight, rushing down the middle of the road with the drivers behind them.

They reached the line of the police. There was a slight scuffle, and then the pigs continued their mad rush to the east, leaving three policemen lying in the dust.

The satisfaction of the people was immense. They shrieked and hugged each other with delight, and it is likely that they will hand down these animals for generations in the tradition of the island.

Two hours later the other party returned, driving three lean cows before them, and a start was made for the slip. At the public-house the policemen were given a drink while the dense crowd that was following waited in the lane. The island bull happened to be in a field close by, and he became wildly excited at the sight of the cows and of the strangely-dressed men. Two young islanders sidled up to me in a moment or two as I was resting on a wall, and one of them whispered in my ear –

'Do you think they could take fines of us if we let out the bull on them?'

In face of the crowd of women and children, I could only say it was probable, and they slunk off.

At the slip there was a good deal of bargaining, which ended in all the cattle being given back to their owners. It was plainly of no use to take them away, as they were worth nothing.

When the last policeman had embarked, an old woman came forward from the crowd and, mounting on a rock near the slip, began a fierce rhapsody in Gaelic, pointing at the bailiff and waving her withered arms with extraordinary rage.

'This man is my own son,' she said; 'it is I that ought to know him. He is the first ruffian in the whole big world.'

Then she gave an account of his life, coloured with a vindictive fury I cannot reproduce. As she went on the excitement became so intense I thought the man would be stoned before he could get back to his cottage.

On these islands the women live only for their children, and it is hard to estimate the power of the impulse that made this old woman stand out and curse her son.

In the fury of her speech I seem to look again into the strangely reticent temperament of the islanders, and to feel the passionate spirit that expresses itself, at odd moments only, with magnificent words and gestures.

Old Pat has told me a story of the goose that lays the golden eggs, which he calls the Phoenix:

A poor widow had three sons and a daughter. One day when her sons were out looking for sticks in the wood they saw a fine speckled bird flying in the trees. The next day they saw it again, and the eldest son told his brothers to go and get sticks by themselves, for he was going after the bird.

He went after it, and brought it in with him when he came home in the evening. They put it in an old hencoop, and they gave it some of the meal they had for themselves; — I don't know if it ate the meal, but they divided what they had themselves; they could do no more.

That night it laid a fine spotted egg in the basket. The next night it laid another.

At that time its name was on the papers and many had heard of the bird that laid the golden eggs, for the eggs were of gold, and there's no lie in it.

When the boys went down to the shop the next day to buy a stone of meal, the shopman asked if he could buy the bird of them. Well, it was arranged in this way. The shopman would marry the boys' sister — a poor simple girl without a stitch of good clothes — and get the bird with her.

Some time after that one of the boys sold an egg of the bird to a gentleman that was in the country. The gentleman asked him if he had the bird still. He said that the man who had married his sister was after getting it.

'Well,' said the gentleman, 'the man who eats the heart of

that bird will find a purse of gold beneath him every morning, and the man who eats its liver will be king of Ireland.'

The boy went out – he was a simple poor fellow – and told the shopman.

Then the shopman brought in the bird and killed it, and he ate the heart himself and he gave the liver to his wife.

When the boy saw that there was great anger on him, and he went back and told the gentleman.

'Do what I'm telling you,' said the gentleman. 'Go down now and tell the shopman and his wife to come up here to play a game of cards with me, for it's lonesome I am this evening.'

When the boy was gone he mixed a vomit and poured the lot of it into a few naggins of whisky, and he put a strong cloth on the table under the cards.

The man came up with his wife and they began to play.

The shopman won the first game and the gentleman made them drink a sup of the whisky.

They played again and the shopman won the second game. Then the gentleman made him drink a sup more of the whisky.

As they were playing the third game the shopman and his wife got sick on the cloth, and the boy picked it up and carried it into the yard, for the gentleman had let him know what he was to do. Then he found the heart of the bird and he ate it, and the next morning when he turned in his bed there was a purse of gold under him.

That is my story.[24]

When the steamer is expected I rarely fail to visit the boat-slip, as the men usually collect when she is in the offing, and lie arguing among their curaghs till she has made her visit to the south island, and is seen coming towards us.

This morning I had a long talk with an old man who was rejoicing over the improvement he has seen here during the last ten or fifteen years.

Till recently there was no communication with the mainland except by hookers, which were usually slow, and could only make the voyage in tolerably fine weather, so that if an islander went to a fair it was often three weeks before he could return. Now, however, the steamer comes here twice in the week, and the voyage is made in three or four hours.

The pier on this island is also a novelty, and is much thought of, as it enables the hookers that still carry turf and cattle to discharge and take their cargoes directly from the shore. The water round it, however, is only deep enough for a hooker when the tide is nearly full, and will never float the steamer, so passengers must still come to land in curaghs.[25] The boat-slip at the corner next the south island is extremely useful in calm weather, but it is exposed to a heavy roll from the south, and is so narrow that the curaghs run some danger of missing it in the tumult of the surf.

In bad weather four men will often stand for nearly an hour at the top of the slip with a curagh in their hands, watching a point of rock towards the south where they can see the strength of the waves that are coming in.

The instant a break is seen they swoop down to the surf, launch their curagh, and pull out to sea with incredible speed. Coming to land is attended with the same difficulty, and, if their moment is badly chosen, they are likely to be washed sideways and swamped among the rocks.

This continual danger, which can only be escaped by extraordinary personal dexterity, has had considerable influence on the local character, as the waves have made it impossible for clumsy, foolhardy, or timid men to live on these islands.

When the steamer is within a mile of the slip, the curaghs are put out and range themselves – there are usually from four to a dozen – in two lines at some distance from the shore.

The moment she comes in among them there is a short but desperate struggle for good places at her side. The men are lolling on their oars talking with the dreamy tone which comes with the rocking of the waves. The steamer lies to, and in an instant their faces become distorted with passion, while the oars bend and quiver with the strain. For one minute they seem utterly indifferent to their own safety and that of their friends and brothers. Then the sequence is decided, and they begin to talk again with the dreamy tone that is habitual to them, while they make fast and clamber up into the steamer.

While the curaghs are out I am left with a few women and very old men who cannot row. One of these old men, whom I often talk with, has some fame as a bone-setter, and is said to have done remarkable cures, both here and on the mainland. Stories are told of how he has been taken off by the quality in their carriages through the hills of Connemara, to treat their sons and daughters, and come home with his pockets full of money.

Another old man, the oldest on the island, is fond of telling me anecdotes – not folk-tales – of things that have happened here in his lifetime.

He often tells me about a Connaught man who killed his father with the blow of a spade when he was in passion, and then fled to this island and threw himself on the mercy of some of the natives with whom he was said to be related. They hid him in a hole – which the old man has shown me – and kept him safe for weeks, though the police came and searched for him, and he could hear their boots grinding on the stones over his head. In spite of a reward which was offered, the island was incorruptible, and after much trouble the man was safely shipped to America.[26]

This impulse to protect the criminal is universal in the west. It seems partly due to the association between justice and the hated English jurisdiction, but more directly to the primitive feeling of these people, who are never criminals yet always capable of crime, that a man will not do wrong unless he is under the influence of a passion which is as irresponsible as a storm on the sea. If a man has killed his father, and is already sick and broken with remorse, they can see no reason why he should be dragged away and killed by the law.

Such a man, they say, will be quiet all the rest of his life, and if you suggest that punishment is needed as an example, they ask, 'Would any one kill his father if he was able to help it?'

Some time ago, before the introduction of police, all the people of the islands were as innocent as the people here remain to this day. I have heard that at that time the ruling proprietor and magistrate of the north island used to give any man who had done wrong a letter to a jailer in Galway, and send him off by himself to serve a term of imprisonment.[27]

As there was no steamer, the ill-doer was given a passage in some chance hooker to the nearest point on the mainland. Then he walked for many miles along a desolate shore till he reached the town. When his time had been put through, he crawled back along the same route, feeble and emaciated, and had often to wait many weeks before he could regain the island. Such at least is the story.

It seems absurd to apply the same laws to these people and to the criminal classes of a city. The most intelligent man on Inishmaan has often spoken to me of his contempt of the law, and of the increase of crime the police have brought to Aranmor. On this island, he says, if men have a little difference, or a little fight, their friends take care it does not go too far, and in a little time it is forgotten. In Kilronan there is a band of men paid to make out cases for themselves; the moment a blow is struck they come down and arrest the man who gave it. The other man he quarrelled with has to give evidence against him; whole families come down to the court and swear against each other till they become bitter enemies. If there is a conviction the man who is convicted never forgives. He waits his time, and before the year is out there is a cross summons, which the other man in turn never forgives. The feud continues to grow, till a dispute about the colour of a man's hair may end in a murder, after a year's forcing by the law. The mere fact that it is impossible to get reliable evidence in the island – not because the people are dishonest, but because they think the claim of kinship more sacred than the claims of abstract truth – turns the whole system of sworn evidence into a demoralizing farce, and it is easy to believe that law dealings on this false basis must lead to every sort of injustice.

While I am discussing these questions with the old men the curaghs begin to come in with cargoes of salt, and flour, and porter.

Today a stir was made by the return of a native who had spent five years in New-York. He came on shore with half a dozen people who had been shopping on the mainland, and walked up and down on the slip in his neat suit, looking strangely foreign to his birthplace, while his old mother of eighty-five ran about on the slippery seaweed, half crazy with delight, telling every one the news.

When the curaghs were in their places the men crowded round him to bid him welcome. He shook hands with them readily enough, but with no smile of recognition.

He is said to be dying.

Yesterday – a Sunday – three young men rowed me over to Inisheer, the south island of the group.

The stern of the curagh was occupied, so I was put in the bow with my head on a level with the gunnel. A considerable sea was running in the sound, and when we came out from the shelter of this island, the curagh rolled and vaulted in a way not easy to describe.

At one moment, as we went down into the furrow, green waves curled and arched themselves above me; then in an instant I was flung up into the air and could look down on the heads of the rowers, as if we were sitting on a ladder, or out across a forest of white crests to the black cliff of Inishmaan.

The men seemed excited and uneasy, and I thought for a moment that we were likely to be swamped. In a little while, however, I realized the capacity of the curagh to raise its head among the waves, and the motion became strangely exhilarating. Even, I thought, if we were dropped into the blue chasm of the waves, this death, with the fresh sea saltness in one's teeth, would be better than most deaths one is likely to meet.

When we reached the other island, it was raining heavily, so that we could not see anything of the antiquities or people.

For the greater part of the afternoon we sat on the tops of empty barrels in the public-house, talking of the destiny of Gaelic. We were admitted as travellers, and the shutters of the shop were closed behind us, letting in only a glimmer of grey light, and the tumult of the storm. Towards evening it cleared a little and we came home in a calmer sea, but with a dead head-wind that gave the rowers all they could do to make the passage.

On calm days I often go out fishing with Michael. When we reach the space above the slip where the curaghs are propped, bottom upwards, on the limestone, he lifts the prow of the one we are going to embark in, and I slip underneath and set the centre of the foremost seat upon my neck. Then he crawls under the stern and stands up with the last seat upon his shoulders. We start for the sea. The long prow bends before me so that I see nothing but a few yards of shingle at my feet. A quivering pain runs from the top of my spine to the sharp stones that seem to pass through my pampooties, and grate upon my ankles. We stagger and groan beneath the weight; but at last our feet reach the slip, and we run down with a half-trot like the pace of barefooted children.

A yard from the sea we stop and lower the curagh to the right. It must be brought down gently – a difficult task for our strained and aching muscles – and sometimes as the gunnel reaches the slip I lose my balance and roll in among the seats.

Yesterday we went out in the curagh that had been damaged on the day of my visit to Kilronan, and as we were putting in the oars the freshly-tarred patch stuck to the slip which was heated with the sunshine. We carried up water in the bailer – the 'cupeen', a shallow wooden vessel like a soup-plate – and with infinite pains we got free and rode away. In a few moments, however, I found the water spouting up at my feet.

The patch had been misplaced, and this time we had no sacking. Michael borrowed my pocket scissors, and with admirable rapidity cut a square of flannel from the tail of his shirt and squeezed it into the hole, making it fast with a splint which he hacked from one of the oars.

During our excitement the tide had carried us to the brink of the rocks, and I admired again the dexterity with which he got his oars into the water and turned us out as we were mounting on a wave that would have hurled us to destruction.

With the injury to our curagh we did not go far from the shore. After a while I took a long spell at the oars, and gained a certain dexterity, though they are not easy to manage. The handles overlap by about six inches – in order to gain leverage, as the curagh is narrow – and at first it is almost impossible to avoid striking the upper oar against one's knuckles. The oars are rough and square, except at the ends, so one cannot do so with impunity. Again, a curagh with two light people in it floats on the water like a nutshell, and the slightest inequality in the stroke throws the prow round at least a right angle from its course. In the first half-hour I found myself more than once moving towards the point I had come from, greatly to Michael's satisfaction.

This morning we were out again near the pier on the north side of the island. As we paddled slowly with the tide, trolling for pollock, several curaghs, weighed to the gunnel with kelp, passed us on their way to Kilronan.

An old woman, rolled in red petticoats, was sitting on a ledge of rock that runs into the sea at the point where the curaghs were passing from the south, hailing them in quavering Gaelic, and asking for a passage to Kilronan.

The first one that came round without a cargo turned in from some distance and took her away.

The morning had none of the supernatural beauty that comes over the island so often in rainy weather, so we basked in the vague enjoyment of the sunshine, looking down at the wild luxuriance of the vegetation beneath the sea, which contrasts strangely with the nakedness above it.

Some dreams I have had in this cottage seem to give strength to the opinion that there is a psychic memory attached to certain neighbourhoods.

Last night, after walking in a dream among buildings with strangely intense light on them, I heard a faint rhythm of music beginning far away on some stringed instrument.

It came closer to me, gradually increasing in quickness and volume with an irresistibly definite progression. When it was quite near the sound began to move in my nerves and blood, and to urge me to dance with them.

I knew that if I yielded I would be carried away to some moment of terrible agony, so I struggled to remain quiet, holding my knees together with my hands.

The music increased continually, sounding like the strings of harps, tuned to a forgotten scale, and having a resonance as searching as the strings of the cello.

Then the luring excitement became more powerful than my will, and my limbs moved in spite of me.

In a moment I was swept away in a whirlwind of notes. My breath and my thoughts and every impulse of my body, became a form of the dance, till I could not distinguish between the instruments and the rhythm and my own person or consciousness.

For a while it seemed an excitement that was filled with joy, then it grew into an ecstasy where all existence was lost in a vortex of movement. I could not think there had ever been a life beyond the whirling of the dance.

Then with a shock the ecstasy turned to an agony and rage. I struggled to free myself, but seemed only to increase the passion of the steps I moved to. When I shrieked I could only echo the notes of the rhythm.

At last with a moment of uncontrollable frenzy I broke back to consciousness and awoke.

I dragged myself trembling to the window of the cottage and looked out. The moon was glittering across the bay, and there was no sound anywhere on the island.

I am leaving in two days, and old Pat Dirane has bidden me goodbye. He met me in the village this morning and took me into 'his little tint', a miserable hovel where he spends the night.

I sat for a long time on his threshold, while he leaned on a stool behind me, near his bed, and told me the last story I shall have from him – a rude anecdote not worth recording. Then he told me with careful emphasis how he had wandered when he was a young man, and lived in a fine college, teaching Irish to the young priests!

They say on the island that he can tell as many lies as four men: perhaps the stories he has learned have strengthened his imagination.

When I stood up in the doorway to give him God's blessing, he leaned over on the straw that forms his bed, and shed tears. Then he turned to me again, lifting up one trembling hand, with the mitten worn to a hole on the palm, from the rubbing of his crutch.

'I'll not see you again,' he said, with tears trickling on his face, 'and you're a kindly man. When you come back next year I won't be in it. I won't live beyond the winter. But listen now to what I'm telling you; let you put insurance on me in the city of Dublin, and it's five hundred pounds you'll get on my burial.'

This evening, my last in the island, is also the evening of the 'Pattern' – a festival something like 'Pardons' of Brittany.[28]

I waited specially to see it, but a piper who was expected did not come, and there was no amusement. A few friends and relations came over from the other island and stood about the public-house in their best clothes, but without music dancing was impossible.

I believe on some occasions when the piper is present there is a fine day of dancing and excitement, but the Galway piper is getting old, and is not easily induced to undertake the voyage.

Last night, St John's Eve, the fires were lighted and boys ran about with pieces of the burning turf, though I could not find out if the idea of lighting the house fires from the bonfire is still found on the island.[29]

I have come out of an hotel full of tourists and commercial travellers, to stroll along the edge of Galway Bay, and look out in the direction of the islands. The sort of yearning I feel towards those lonely rocks is indescribably acute. This town, that is usually so full of wild human interest, seems in my present mood a tawdry medley of all that is crudest in modern life. The nullity of the rich and the squalor of the poor give me the same pang of wondering disgust; yet the islands are fading already and I can hardly realize that the smell of the seaweed and the drone of the Atlantic are still moving round them.

One of my island friends has written to me:

Dear John Synge, – I am for a long time expecting a letter from you and I think you are forgetting this island altogether.

Mr — died a long time ago on the big island and his boat

was on anchor in the harbour and the wind blew her to Black Head and broke her up after his death.

Tell me are you learning Irish since you went. We have a branch of the Gaelic league[30] here now and the people is going on well with the Irish and reading.

I will write the next letter in Irish to you. Tell me will you come to see us next year and if you will you'll write a letter before you. All your loving friends is well in health. – *Mise do chara go buan.*[31]

Another boy I sent some baits to has written to me also, beginning his letter in Irish and ending it in English:

Dear John, – I got your letter four days ago, and there was pride and joy on me because it was written in Irish, and a fine, good, pleasant letter it was. The baits you sent are very good, but I lost two of them and half of my line. A big fish came and caught the bait, and the line was bad and half of the line and the baits went away. My sister has come back from America, but I'm thinking it won't be long till she goes away again, for it is lonesome and poor she finds the island now. – I am your friend . . .

Write soon and let you write in Irish, if you don't I won't look on it.

PART II

The evening before I returned to the west I wrote to Michael – who had left the islands to earn his living on the mainland – to tell him that I would call at the house where he lodged the next morning, which was a Sunday.

A young girl with fine western features, and little English, came out when I knocked at the door. She seemed to have heard all about me, and was so filled with the importance of her message that she could hardly speak it intelligibly.

'She got your letter,' she said, confusing the pronouns, as is often done in the west, 'she is gone to Mass, and she'll be in the square after that. Let your honour go now and sit in the square and Michael will find you.'

As I was returning up the main street I met Michael wandering down to meet me, as he had got tired of waiting.

He seemed to have grown a powerful man since I had seen him, and was now dressed in the heavy brown flannels of the Connaught labourer. After a little talk we turned back together and went out on the sandhills above the town. Meeting him here a little beyond the threshold of my hotel I was singularly struck with the refinement of his nature, which has hardly been influenced by his new life, and the townsmen and sailors he has met with.

'I do often come outside the town on Sunday,' he said while we were talking, 'for what is there to do in a town in the middle of all the people when you are not at your work?'

A little later another Irish-speaking labourer – a friend of Michael's – joined us, and we lay for hours talking and arguing on the grass. The day was unbearably sultry, and the sand and the sea near us were crowded with half-naked women, but neither of the young men seemed to be aware of their presence. Before we went back to the town a man came out to ring a young horse on the sand close to where we were lying, and then the interest of my companions was intense.

Late in the evening I met Michael again, and we wandered round the bay, which was still filled with bathing women, until it was quite dark. I shall not see him again before my return from the islands, as he is busy tomorrow, and on Tuesday I go out with the steamer.

I returned to the middle island this morning, in the steamer to Kilronan, and on here in a curagh that had gone over with salt fish. As I came up from the slip the doorways in the village filled with women and children, and several came down on the roadway to shake hands and bid me a thousand welcomes.

Old Pat Dirane is dead, and several of my friends have gone to America; that is all the news they have to give me after an absence of many months.

When I arrived at the cottage I was welcomed by the old people, and great excitement was made by some little presents I had bought them – a pair of folding scissors for the old woman, a strop for her husband, and some other trifles.

Then the youngest son, Columb, who is still at home, went into the inner room and brought out the alarm clock I sent them last year when I went away.

'I am very fond of this clock,' he said, patting it on the back; 'it will ring for me any morning when I want to go out fishing. Bedad, there are no two cocks in the island that would be equal to it.'

I had some photographs to show them that I took here last year, and while I was sitting on a little stool near the door of the kitchen, showing them to the family, a beautiful young woman I had spoken to a few times last year slipped in, and after a wonderfully simple and cordial speech of welcome, she sat down on the floor beside me to look on also.

The complete absence of shyness or self-consciousness in most of these people gives them a peculiar charm, and when this young and beautiful woman leaned across my knees to look nearer at some photograph that pleased her, I felt more than ever the strange simplicity of the island life.

Last year when I came here everything was new, and the people were a little strange with me, but now I am familiar with them and their way of life, so that their qualities strike me more forcibly than before.

When my photographs of this island had been examined with immense delight, and every person in them had been identified – even those who only showed a hand or a leg – I brought out some I had taken in County Wicklow. Most of them were fragments, showing fairs in Rathdrum or Aughrim, men cutting turf on the hills, or other scenes of inland life, yet they gave the greatest delight to these people who are wearied of the sea.

This year I see a darker side of life in the islands. The sun seldom shines, and day after day a cold south-western wind blows over the cliffs, bringing up showers of hail and dense masses of cloud.

The sons who are at home stay out fishing whenever it is tolerably calm, from about three in the morning till after night-fall, yet they earn little, as fish are not plentiful.

The old man fishes also with a long rod and ground-bait, but as a rule has even smaller success.

When the weather breaks completely, fishing is abandoned, and they both go down and dig potatoes in the rain. The women sometimes help them, but their usual work is to look after the calves and do their spinning in the house.

There is a vague depression over the family this year, because of the two sons who have gone away, Michael to the mainland and another son, who was working in Kilronan last year, to the United States.

A letter came yesterday from Michael to his mother. It was written in English, as he is the only one of the family who can read or write in Irish, and I heard it being slowly spelled out and translated as I sat in my room. A little later the old woman brought it in for me to read.

He told her first about his work, and the wages he is getting. Then he said that one night he had been walking in the town, and had looked up among the streets, and thought to himself what a grand night it would be on the Sandy Head of this island – not, he added, that he was feeling lonely or sad. At the end he gave an account, with the dramatic emphasis of the folk-tale, of how he had met me on the Sunday morning, and, 'believe me', he said, 'it was the fine talk we had for two hours or three'. He told them also of a knife I had given him that was so fine, no one on the island 'had ever seen the like of her'.

Another day a letter came from the son who is in America, to say that he had had a slight accident to one of his arms, but was well again, and that he was leaving New York and going a few hundred miles up the country.

All the evening afterwards the old woman sat on her stool at the corner of the fire with her shawl over her head, keening piteously to herself. America appeared far away, yet she seems to have felt that, after all, it was only the other edge of the Atlantic, and now when she hears them talking of railroads and inland cities where there is no sea, things she cannot understand, it comes home to her that her son is gone for ever. She often tells me how she used to sit on the wall behind the house last year and watch the hooker he worked in coming out of Kilronan and beating up the sound, and what company it used to be to her the time they'd all be out.

The maternal feeling is so powerful on these islands that it gives a life of torment to the women. Their sons grow up to be banished as soon as they are of age, or to live here in continual danger on the sea; their daughters go away also, or are worn out in their youth with bearing children that grow up to harass them in their own turn a little later.

There has been a storm for the last twenty-four hours, and I have been wandering on the cliffs till my hair is stiff with salt. Immense masses of spray were flying up from the base of the cliff, and were caught at times by the wind and whirled away to fall at some distance from the shore. When one of these happened to fall on me, I had to crouch down for an instant, wrapped and blinded by a white hail of foam.

The waves were so enormous that when I saw one more than usually large coming towards me, I turned instinctively to hide myself, as one blinks when struck upon the eyes.

After a few hours the mind grows bewildered with the

endless change and struggle of the sea, and an utter despondency replaces the first moment of exhilaration.

At the south-west corner of the island I came upon a number
of people gathering the seaweed that is now thick on the rocks.
It was raked from the surf by the men, and then carried up to
the brow of the cliff by a party of young girls.

In addition to their ordinary clothing these girls wore a raw
sheepskin on their shoulders, to catch the oozing sea water,
and they looked strangely wild and seal-like with the salt caked
upon their lips and wreaths of seaweed in their hair.

For the rest of my walk I saw no living thing but one flock
of curlews, and a few pipits hiding among the stones.

About the sunset the clouds broke and the storm turned to a
hurricane. Bars of purple cloud stretched across the sound
where immense waves were rolling from the west, wreathed
with snowy phantasies of spray. Then there was the bay full of
green delirium, and the Twelve Pins touched with mauve and
scarlet in the east.

The suggestion from this world of inarticulate power was
immense, and now at midnight, when the wind is abating, I
am still trembling and flushed with exultation.

I have been walking through the wet lanes in my pampooties
in spite of the rain, and I have brought on a feverish cold.

The wind is terrific. If anything serious should happen to
me I might die here and be nailed in my box, and shoved
down into a wet crevice in the graveyard before any one could
know it on the mainland.

Two days ago a curagh passed from the south island – they
can go out when we are weather-bound because of a sheltered
cove in their island – it was thought in search of the Doctor. It
became too rough afterwards to make the return journey, and
it was only this morning we saw them repassing towards the
south-east in a terrible sea.

A four-oared curagh with two men in her besides the rowers
– probably the Priest and the Doctor – went first, followed by
the three-oared curagh from the south island, which ran more
danger. Often when they go for the Doctor in weather like

this, they bring the Priest also, as they do not know if it will be possible to go for him if he is needed later.

As a rule there is little illness, and the women often manage their confinements among themselves without any trained assistance. In most cases all goes well, but at times a curagh is sent off in desperate haste for the Priest and the Doctor when it is too late.

The baby that spent some days here last year is now established in the house; I suppose the old woman has adopted him to console herself for the loss of her own sons.

He is now a well-grown child, though not yet able to say more than a few words of Gaelic. His favourite amusement is to stand behind the door with a stick, waiting for any wandering pig or hen that may chance to come in, and then to dash out and pursue them. There are two young kittens in the kitchen also, which he ill-treats, without meaning to do them harm.

Whenever the old woman comes into my room with turf for the fire, he walks in solemnly behind her with a sod under each arm, deposits them on the back of the fire with great care, and then flies off round the corner with his long petticoats trailing behind him.

He has not yet received any official name on the island, as he has not left the fireside, but in the house they usually speak of him as 'Micilín Beag' (i.e., 'little small-Michael').

Now and then he is slapped, but for the most part the old woman keeps him in order with stories of 'the long-toothed hag', that lives in the Dun and eats children who are not good. He spends half his day eating cold potatoes and drinking very strong tea, yet seems in perfect health.

An Irish letter has come to me from Michael. I will translate it literally.

Dear noble Person[32] – I write this letter with joy and pride that you found the way to the house of my father the day you were on the steamship. I am thinking there will not be loneliness on you, for there will be the fine beautiful Gaelic League and you will be learning powerfully.

I am thinking there is no one in life walking with you now but your own self from morning till night, and great is the pity.

What way are my mother and my three brothers and my sisters, and do not forget white Michael, and the poor little child and the old grey woman, and Rory. I am getting a forgetfulness on all my friends and kindred. – I am your friend . . .

It is curious how he accuses himself of forgetfulness after asking for all his family by name. I suppose the first homesickness is wearing away and he looks on his independent wellbeing as a treason towards his kindred.

One of his friends was in the kitchen when the letter was brought to me, and, by the old man's wish, he read it out loud as soon as I had finished it. When he came to the last sentence he hesitated for a moment, and then omitted it altogether.

This young man had come up to bring me a copy of the *Love Songs of Connaught*, which he possesses, and I persuaded him to read, or rather chant me some of them.[33] When he had read a couple I found that the old woman knew many of them from her childhood, though her version was often not the same as what was in the book. She was rocking herself on a stool in the chimney corner beside a pot of indigo, in which she was dyeing wool, and several times when the young man finished a poem she took it up again and recited the verses with exquisite musical intonation, putting a wistfulness and passion into her voice that seemed to give it all the cadences that are sought in the profoundest poetry.

The lamp had burned low, and another terrible gale was howling and shrieking over the island. It seemed like a dream that I should be sitting here among these men and women listening to this rude and beautiful poetry that is filled with the oldest passions of the world.

The horses have been coming back for the last few days from their summer's grazing in Connemara. They are landed at the sandy beach where the cattle were shipped last year, and I went down early this morning to watch their arrival through the waves. The hooker was anchored at some distance from the shore, but I could see a horse standing at the gunnel surrounded by men shouting and flipping at it with bits of rope. In a moment it jumped over into the sea, and some men, who were waiting for it in a curagh, caught it by the halter and towed it to within twenty yards of the surf. Then the curagh turned back to the hooker, and the horse was left to make its own way to the land.

As I was standing about a man came up to me and asked after the usual salutations:

'Is there any war in the world at this time, noble person?'

I told him something of the excitement in the Transvaal, and then another horse came near the waves and I passed on and left him.

Afterwards I walked round the edge of the sea to the pier, where a quantity of turf has recently been brought in. It is usually left for some time stacked on the sandhills, and then carried up to the cottages in panniers slung on donkeys or any horses that are on the island.

They have been busy with it the last few weeks, and the track from the village to the pier has been filled with lines of red-petticoated boys driving their donkeys before them, or cantering down on their backs when the panniers are empty.

In some ways these men and women seem strangely far away from me. They have the same emotions that I have, and the animals have, yet I cannot talk to them when there is much to say, more than to the dog that whines beside me in a mountain fog.

There is hardly an hour I am with them that I do not feel the shock of some inconceivable idea, and then again the shock of some vague emotion that is familiar to them and to me. On some days I feel this island as a perfect home and resting place; on other days I feel that I am a waif among the people. I can feel more with them than they can feel with me, and while I wander among them, they like me sometimes, and laugh at me sometimes, yet never know what I am doing.

In the evenings I sometimes meet with a girl who is not yet

half through her teens, yet seems in some ways more consciously developed than any one else that I have met here. She has passed part of her life on the mainland, and the disillusion she found in Galway has coloured her imagination.

As we sit on stools on either side of the fire I hear her voice going backwards and forwards in the same sentence from the gaiety of a child to the plaintive intonation of an old race that is worn with sorrow. At one moment she is a simple peasant, at another she seems to be looking out at the world with a sense of prehistoric disillusion and to sum up in the expression of her grey-blue eyes the whole external despondency of the clouds and sea.

Our conversation is usually disjointed. One evening we talked of a town on the mainland.

'Ah, it's a queer place,' she said; 'I wouldn't choose to live in it. It's a queer place, and indeed I don't know the place that isn't.'

Another evening we talked of the people who live on the island or come to visit it.

'Father — is gone,' she said; 'he was a kind man but a queer man. Priests is queer people, and I don't know who isn't.'

Then after a long pause she told me with seriousness, as if speaking of a thing that surprised herself, and should surprise me, that she was very fond of the boys.

In our talk, which is sometimes full of the innocent realism of childhood, she is always pathetically eager to say the right thing and be engaging.

One evening I found her trying to light a fire in the little side room of her cottage, where there is an ordinary fireplace. I went in to help her and showed her how to hold up a paper before the mouth of the chimney to make a draught, a method she had never seen. Then I told her of men who live alone in Paris and make their own fires that they may have no one to bother them. She was sitting in a heap on the floor staring into the turf, and as I finished she looked up with surprise.

'They're like me so,' she said; 'would any one have thought that!'

Below the sympathy we feel there is still a chasm between us.

'Musha,' she muttered as I was leaving her this evening, 'I think it's to hell you'll be going by and by.'

Occasionally I meet her also in a kitchen where young men go to play cards after dark and a few girls slip in to share the amusement. At such times her eyes shine in the light of the candles, and her cheeks flush with the first tumult of youth, till she hardly seems the same girl who sits every evening droning to herself over the turf.

A branch of the Gaelic League has been started here since my last visit, and every Sunday afternoon three little girls walk through the village ringing a shrill hand-bell, as a signal that the women's meeting[34] is to be held – here it would be useless to fix an hour, as the hours are not recognized.

Soon afterwards bands of girls – of all ages from five to twenty-five – begin to troop down to the schoolhouse in their reddest Sunday petticoats. It is remarkable that these young women are willing to spend their one afternoon of freedom in laborious studies of orthography for no reason but a vague reverence for the Gaelic. It is true that they owe this reverence, or most of it, to the influence of some recent visitors, yet the fact that they feel such an influence so keenly is itself of interest.

In the older generation that did not come under the influence of the recent language movement, I do not see any particular affection for Gaelic. Whenever they are able, they speak English to their children, to render them more capable of making their way in life. Even the young men sometimes say to me –

'There's very hard English on you, and I wish to God that I had the like of it.'

The women are the great conservative force in this matter of the language. They learn a little English in school and from their parents, but they rarely have occasion to speak with any one who is not a native of the islands, so their knowledge of the foreign tongue remains rudimentary. In my cottage I have never heard a word of English from the women except when they were speaking to the pigs or to the dogs, or when the girl was reading a letter in English. Women, however, with a more assertive temperament, who have had, apparently, the same opportunities, often attain a considerable fluency, as is the case with one, a relative of the old woman of the house, who often visits here.

In the boys' school, where I sometimes look in, the children surprise me by their knowledge of English, though they always speak in Irish among themselves. The school itself is a comfortless building in a terribly bleak position. In cold weather the children arrive in the morning with a sod of turf tied up with their books, a simple toll which keeps the fire well supplied, yet, I believe, a more modern method is soon to be introduced.

I am in the north island again, looking out with a singular sensation to the cliffs across the sound. It is hard to believe that those hovels I can just see in the south are filled with people whose lives have the strange quality that is found in the oldest poetry and legend. Compared with them the falling off that has come with the increased prosperity of this island is full of discouragement. The charm which the people over there share with the birds and flowers has been replaced here by the anxiety of men who are eager for gain. The eyes and expression are different, though the faces are the same, and even the children here seem to have an indefinable modern quality that is absent from the men of Inishmaan.

My voyage from the middle island was wild. The morning was so stormy, that in ordinary circumstances I would not have attempted the passage, but as I had arranged to travel with a curagh that was coming over for the Parish Priest – who is to hold stations[35] on Inishmaan – I did not like to draw back.

I went out in the morning and walked up to the cliffs as usual. Several men I fell in with shook their heads when I told them I was going away, and said they doubted if a curagh could cross the sound with the sea that was in it.

When I went back to the cottage I found the Curate had just come across from the south island, and had had a worse passage than any he had yet experienced.

The tide was to turn at two o'clock, and after that it was

thought the sea would be calmer, as the wind and the waves would be running from the same point. We sat about in the kitchen all the morning, with men coming in every few minutes to give their opinion whether the passage should be attempted, and at what points the sea was likely to be at its worst.

At last it was decided we should go, and I started for the pier in a wild shower of rain with the wind howling in the walls. The schoolmaster and a priest who was to have gone with me came out as I was passing through the village and advised me not to make the passage; but my crew had gone on towards the sea, and I thought it better to go after them. The eldest son of the family was coming with me, and I considered that the old man, who knew the waves better than I did, would not send out his son if there was more than reasonable danger.

I found my crew waiting for me under a high wall below the village, and we went on together. The island had never seemed so desolate. Looking out over the black limestone through the driving rain to the gulf of struggling waves, an indescribable feeling of dejection came over me.

The old man gave me his view of the use of fear.

'A man who is not afraid of the sea will soon be drownded,' he said, 'for he will be going out on a day he shouldn't. But we do be afraid of the sea, and we do only be drownded now and again.'

A little crowd of neighbours had collected lower down to see me off, and as we crossed the sandhills we had to shout to each other to be heard above the wind.

The crew carried down the curagh and then stood under the lee of the pier tying on their hats with string and drawing on their oilskins.

They tested the braces of the oars, and the oarpins, and everything in the curagh with a care I had not yet seen them give to anything, then my bag was lifted in, and we were ready. Besides the four men of the crew a man was going with us who wanted a passage to this island. As he was scrambling into the bow, an old man stood forward from the crowd.

'Don't take that man with you,' he said. 'Last week they were taking him to Clare and the whole of them were near drownded. Another day he went to Inisheer and they broke three ribs of the curagh, and they coming back. There is not the like of him for ill-luck in the three islands.'

'The divil choke your old gob,' said the man, 'you will be talking.'

We set off. It was a four-oared curagh, and I was given the last seat so as to leave the stern for the man who was steering with an oar, worked at right angles to the others by an extra thole-pin in the stern gunnel.

When we had gone about a hundred yards they ran up a bit of a sail in the bow and the pace became extraordinarily rapid.

The shower had passed over and the wind had fallen, but large, magnificently brilliant waves were rolling down on us at right angles to our course.

Every instant the steersman whirled us round with a sudden stroke of his oar, the prow reared up and then fell into the next furrow with a crash, throwing up masses of spray. As it did so, the stern in its turn was thrown up, and both the steersman, who let go his oar and clung with both hands to the gunnel, and myself, were lifted high up above the sea.

The wave passed, we regained our course and rowed violently for a few yards, when the same manoeuvre had to be repeated. As we worked out into the sound we began to meet another class of waves, that could be seen for some distance towering above the rest.

When one of these came in sight, the first effort was to get beyond its reach. The steersman began crying out in Gaelic 'Siúil, Siúil' ('Run, run'), and sometimes, when the mass was gliding towards us with horrible speed, his voice rose to a shriek. Then the rowers themselves took up the cry, and the curagh seemed to leap and quiver with the frantic terror of a beast till the wave passed behind it or fell with a crash beside the stern.

It was in this racing with the waves that our chief danger lay. If the wave could be avoided, it was better to do so, but if it overtook us while we were trying to escape, and caught us on the broadside, our destruction was certain. I could see the steersman quivering with the excitement of his task, for any error in his judgement would have swamped us.

We had one narrow escape. A wave appeared high above the rest, and there was the usual moment of intense exertion. It was of no use, and in an instant the wave seemed to be hurling itself upon us. With a yell of rage the steersman struggled with his oar to bring our prow to meet it. He had almost succeeded, when there was a crash and rush of water round us. I felt as if I had been struck upon the back with knotted ropes. White foam gurgled round my knees and eyes. The curagh reared up, swaying and trembling for a moment, and then fell safely into the furrow.

This was our worst moment, though more than once, when several waves came so closely together that we had no time to regain control of the canoe between them, we had some dangerous work. Our lives depended upon the skill and courage of the men, as the life of the rider or swimmer is often in his own hands, and the excitement of the struggle was too great to allow time for fear.

I enjoyed the passage. Down in this shallow trough of canvas that bent and trembled with the motion of the men, I had a far more intimate feeling of the glory and power of the waves than I have ever known in a steamer.

Old Máirtín is keeping me company again, and I am now able to understand the greater part of his Irish.

He took me out today to show me the remains of some cloghauns, or beehive dwellings, that are left near the central ridge of the island. After I had looked at them we lay down in the corner of a little field, filled with the autumn sunshine and the odour of withering flowers, while he told me a long folk-tale which took more than an hour to narrate.

He is so blind that I can gaze at him without discourtesy, and after a while the expression of his face made me forget to listen, and I lay dreamily in the sunshine letting the antique formulas of the story blend with the suggestions from the prehistoric masonry I lay on. The glow of childish transport that came over him when he reached the nonsense ending – so common in these tales – recalled me to myself, and I listened attentively while he gabbled with delighted haste: 'They found the path and I found the puddle. They were drowned and I was found. If it's all one to me tonight, it wasn't all one to them the next night. Yet, if it wasn't itself, not a thing did they lose but an old back tooth' – or some such gibberish.

As I led him home through the paths he described to me – it is thus we get along – lifting him at times over the low walls he is too shaky to climb, he brought the conversation to the topic they are never weary of – my views on marriage.

He stopped as we reached the summit of the island, with the stretch of the Atlantic just visible behind him.

'Whisper, noble person,' he began, 'do you never be thinking on the young girls? The time I was a young man, the divil a one of them could I look on without wishing to marry her.'

'Ah, Máirtín,' I answered, 'it's great wonder you'd be asking me. What at all do you think of me yourself?'

'Bedad, noble person, I'm thinking it's soon you'll be getting married. Listen to what I'm telling you: a man who is not married is no better than an old jackass. He goes into his sister's house, and into his brother's house; he eats a bit in this place and a bit in another place, but he has no home for himself; like an old jackass straying on the rock.'

I have left Aran. The steamer had a more than usually heavy cargo, and it was after four o'clock when we sailed from Kilronan.

Again I saw the three low rocks sink down into the sea with a moment of inconceivable distress. It was a clear evening, and as we came out into the bay the sun stood like an aureole behind the cliffs of Inishmaan. A little later a brilliant glow came over the sky, throwing out the blue of the sea and of the hills of Connemara.

When it was quite dark, the cold became intense, and I wandered about the lonely vessel that seemed to be making her own way across the sea. I was the only passenger, and all the crew, except one boy who was steering, were huddled together in the warmth of the engine-room.

Three hours passed, and no one stirred. The slowness of the vessel and the lamentation of the cold sea about her sides became almost unendurable. Then the lights of Galway came in sight, and the crew appeared as we beat up slowly to the quay.

Once on shore I had some difficulty in finding any one to carry my baggage to the railway. When I found a man in the darkness and got my bag on his shoulders, he turned out to be drunk, and I had trouble to keep him from rolling from the wharf with all my possessions. He professed to be taking me by a short cut into the town, but when we were in the middle of a waste of broken buildings and skeletons of ships he threw my bag on the ground and sat down on it.

'It's real heavy she is, your honour,' he said; 'I'm thinking it's gold there will be in it.'

'Divil a hap'worth is there in it at all but books,' I answered him in Gaelic.

'Bedad, is mór an trua é' ('It's a big pity'), he said; 'if it was gold was in it it's the thundering spree we'd have together this night in Galway.'

In about half an hour I got my luggage once more on his back, and we made our way into the city.

Later in the evening I went down towards the quay to look for Michael. As I turned into the narrow street where he lodges, some one seemed to be following me in the shadow, and when I stopped to find the number of his house I heard the 'Fáilte' (Welcome) of Inishmaan pronounced close to me.

It was Michael.

'I saw you in the street,' he said, 'but I was ashamed to speak to you in the middle of the people, so I followed you the way I'd see if you'd remember me.'

We turned back together and walked about the town till he had to go to his lodgings. He was still just the same, with all his old simplicity and shrewdness; but the work he has here does not agree with him, and he is not contented.

It was the eve of the Parnell celebration in Dublin, and the town was full of excursionists waiting for a train which was to start at midnight.[36] When Michael left me I spent some time in an hotel, and then wandered down to the railway.

A wild crowd was on the platform, surging round the train

in every stage of intoxication. It gave me a better instance than I had yet seen of the half-savage temperament of Connaught. The tension of human excitement seemed greater in this insignificant crowd than anything I have felt among enormous mobs in Rome or Paris.

There were a few people from the islands on the platform, and I got in along with them to a third-class carriage. One of the women of the party had her niece with her, a young girl from Connaught who was put beside me; at the other end of the carriage there were some old men who were talking in Irish, and a young man who had been a sailor.

When the train started there were wild cheers and cries on the platform, and in the train itself the noise was intense; men and women shrieking and singing and beating their sticks on the partitions. At several stations there was a rush to the bar, so the excitement increased as we proceeded.

At Ballinasloe there were some soldiers on the platform looking for places. The sailor in our compartment had a dispute with one of them, and in an instant the door was flung open and the compartment was filled with reeling uniforms and sticks. Peace was made after a moment of uproar and the soldiers got out, but as they did so a pack of their women followers thrust their bare heads and arms into the doorway, cursing and blaspheming with extraordinary rage.

As the train moved away a moment later, these women set up a frantic lamentation. I looked out and caught a glimpse of the wildest heads and figures I have ever seen, shrieking and screaming and waving their naked arms in the light of the lanterns.

As the night went on girls began crying out in the carriage next us, and I could hear the words of obscene songs when the train stopped at a station.

In our own compartment the sailor would allow no one to sleep, and talked all night with sometimes a touch of wit or brutality, and always with a wonderful fluency with wild temperament behind it.

The old men in the corner, dressed in black coats that had something of the antiquity of heirlooms, talked all night among themselves in Gaelic. The young girl beside me lost her shyness after a while, and let me point out the features of the country that were beginning to appear through the dawn as we drew nearer Dublin. She was delighted with the shadows of the trees – trees are rare in Connaught – and with the canal, which was beginning to reflect the morning light. Every time I showed her some new shadow she cried out with naïve excitement –

'Oh, it's lovely, but I can't see it.'

This presence at my side contrasted curiously with the brutality that shook the barrier behind us. The whole spirit of the west of Ireland, with its strange wildness and reserve, seemed moving in this single train to pay a last homage to the dead statesman of the east.

PART III

A letter has come from Michael while I am in Paris. It is in English.

My dear Friend, – I hope that you are in good health since I have heard from you before, its many a time I do think of you since and it was not forgetting you I was for the future.

I was at home in the beginning of March for a fortnight and was very bad with the Influence, but I took good care of myself.

I am getting good wages from the first of this year, and I am afraid I won't be able to stand with it, although it is not hard, I am working in a saw-mills and getting the money for the wood and keeping an account of it.

I am getting a letter and some news from home two or three times a week, and they are all well in health, and your friends in the island as well as if I mentioned them.

Did you see any of my friends in Dublin Mr — or any of those gentlemen or gentlewomen.

I think I soon try America but not until next year if I am alive.

I hope we might meet again in good and pleasant health.

It is now time to come to a conclusion, goodbye and not for ever, write soon. – I am your friend in Galway.

Write soon dear friend.

Another letter in a more rhetorical mood.

Mr dear Mr S., – I am for a long time trying to spare a little time for to write a few words to you.

Hoping that you are still considering good and pleasant health since I got a letter from you before.

I see now that your time is coming round to come to this place to learn your native language. There was a great Feis[37]

in this island two weeks ago, and there was a very large attendance from the South island, and not very many from the
North.

Two cousins of my own have been in this house for three
weeks or beyond it, but now they are gone, and there is a place
for you if you wish to come, and you can write before you and
we'll try and manage you as well as we can.

I am at home now for about two months, for the mill was
burnt where I was at work. After that I was in Dublin, but I
did not get my health in that city. – *Mise le mór mheas ort a
chara.*[38]

Soon after I received this letter I wrote to Michael to say
that I was going back to them. This time I chose a day when
the steamer went direct to the middle island, and as we came
up between the two lines of curaghs that were waiting outside
the slip, I saw Michael, dressed once more in his island clothes,
rowing in one of them.

He made no sign of recognition, but as soon as they could
get alongside he clambered on board and came straight up on
the bridge to where I was.

'Bhfuil tú go maith?' ('Are you well?') he said. 'Where is
your bag?'

His curagh had got a bad place near the bow of the steamer,
so I was slung down from a considerable height on top of some
sacks of flour and my own bag, while the curagh swayed and
battered itself against the side.

When we were clear I asked Michael if he had got my letter.

'Ah no,' he said, 'not a sight of it, but maybe it will come
next week.'

Part of the slip had been washed away during the winter, so
we had to land to the left of it, among the rocks, taking our
turn with the other curaghs that were coming in.

As soon as I was on shore the men crowded round me to bid
me welcome, asking me as they shook hands if I had travelled
far in the winter, and seen many wonders, ending, as usual,
with the inquiry if there was much war at present in the world.

It gave me a thrill of delight to hear their Gaelic blessings, and to see the steamer moving away, leaving me quite alone among them. The day was fine with a clear sky, and the sea was glittering beyond the limestone. Further off a light haze on the cliffs of the larger island, and on the Connaught hills, gave me the illusion that it was still summer.

A little boy was sent off to tell the old woman that I was coming, and we followed slowly talking, and carrying the baggage.

When I had exhausted my news they told me theirs. A power of strangers – four or five – a French priest among them, had been on the island in the summer; the potatoes were bad, but the rye had begun well, till a dry week came and then it had turned into oats.

'If you didn't know us so well,' said the man who was talking, 'you'd think it was a lie we were telling, but the sorrow a lie is in it. It grew straight and well till it was as high as your knee, then it turned into oats. Did ever you see the like of that in County Wicklow?'

In the cottage everything was as usual, but Michael's presence has brought back the old woman's humour and contentment. As I sat down on my stool and lit my pipe with the corner of a sod, I could have cried out with the feeling of festivity that this return procured me.

This year Michael is busy in the daytime, but at present there is a harvest moon, and we spend most of the evening wandering about the island, looking out over the bay where the shadows of the clouds throw strange patterns of gold and black. As we were returning through the village this evening a tumult of revelry broke out from one of the smaller cottages, and Michael said it was the young boys and girls who have sport at this time of the year. I would have liked to join them, but feared to embarrass their amusement. When we passed on again the groups of scattered cottages on each side of the way reminded me of places I have sometimes passed when travelling at night in France or Bavaria, places that seemed so enshrined in the blue silence of night one could not believe they would reawaken.

Afterwards we went up on the Dun, where Michael said he had never been before after nightfall, though he lives within a stone's-throw. The place gains unexpected grandeur in this light, standing out like a corona of prehistoric stone upon the summit of the island. We walked round the top of the wall for some time looking down on the faint yellow roofs, with the rocks glittering beyond them, and the silence of the bay. Though Michael is sensible of the beauty of the nature round him, he never speaks of it directly, and many of our evening walks are occupied with long Gaelic discourses about the movements of the stars and moon.

These people make no distinction between the natural and the supernatural.

This afternoon – it was Sunday, when there is usually some interesting talk among the islanders – it rained, so I went into the schoolmaster's kitchen, which is a good deal frequented by the more advanced among the people. I know so little of their ways of fishing and farming that I do not find it easy to keep up our talk without reaching matters where they cannot follow me, and since the novelty of my photographs has passed off I have some difficulty in giving them the entertainment they seem to expect from my company. Today I showed them some simple gymnastic feats and conjurer's tricks, which gave them great amusement.

'Tell us now,' said an old woman when I had finished, 'didn't you learn those things from the witches that do be out in the country?'

In one of the tricks I seemed to join a piece of string which was cut by the people, and the illusion was so complete that I saw one man going off with it into the corner and pulling at the apparent joining till he sank red furrows round his hands.

Then he brought it back to me.

'Bedad,' he said, 'this is the greatest wonder ever I seen. The cord is a taste thinner where you joined it but as strong as ever it was.'

A few of the younger men look doubtful, but the older people, who have watched the rye turning into oats, seemed to accept the magic frankly, and did not show any surprise that a 'duine uasal' (a noble person) should be able to do like the witches.

My intercourse with these people has made me realize that miracles must abound wherever the new conception of law is not understood. On these islands alone miracles enough happen every year to equip a divine emissary. Rye is turned into oats, storms are raised to keep evictors from the shore, cows that are isolated on lonely rocks bring forth calves, and other things of the same kind are common.

The wonder is a rare expected event, like the thunderstorm or the rainbow, except that it is a little rarer and a little more wonderful. Often, when I am walking and get into conversation with some of the people, and tell them that I have received a paper from Dublin, they ask me –

'And is there any great wonder in the world at this time?'

When I had finished my feats of dexterity, I was surprised to find that none of the islanders, even the youngest and most agile, could do what I did. As I pulled their limbs about in my effort to teach them, I felt that the ease and beauty of their movements has made me think them lighter than they really are. Seen in their curaghs between these cliffs and the Atlantic, they appear lithe and small, but if they were dressed as we are and seen in an ordinary room, many of them would seem heavily and powerfully made.

One man, however, the champion dancer of the island, got up after a while and displayed the salmon leap – lying flat on his face and then springing up, horizontally, high in the air – and some other feats of extraordinary agility, but he is not young and we could not get him to dance.

In the evening I had to repeat my tricks here in the kitchen, for the fame of them had spread over the island.

No doubt these feats will be remembered here for generations. The people have so few images for description that they seize on anything that is remarkable in their visitors and use it afterwards in their talk.

For the last few years when they are speaking of any one with fine rings they say: 'She had beautiful rings on her fingers like Lady — ,' a visitor to the island.

*

I have been down sitting on the pier till it was quite dark. I am only beginning to understand the nights of Inishmaan and the influence they have had in giving distinction to these men who do most of their work after nightfall.

I could hear nothing but a few curlews and other wild-fowl whistling and shrieking in the seaweed, and the low rustling of the waves. It was one of the dark sultry nights peculiar to September, with no light anywhere except the phosphorescence of the sea, and an occasional rift in the clouds that showed the stars behind them.

The sense of solitude was immense. I could not see or realize my own body, and I seemed to exist merely in my perception of the waves and of the crying birds, and of the smell of seaweed.

When I tried to come home I lost myself among the sandhills, and the night seemed to grow unutterably cold and dejected, as I groped among slimy masses of seaweed and wet crumbling walls.

After a while I heard a movement in the sand, and two grey shadows appeared beside me. They were two men who were going home from fishing. I spoke to them and knew their voices, and we went home together.

In the autumn season the threshing of the rye is one of the many tasks that fall to the men and boys. The sheaves are collected on a bare rock, and then each is beaten separately on a couple of stones placed on end one against the other. The land is so poor that a field hardly produces more grain than is needed for seed the following year, so the rye-growing is carried on merely for the straw, which is used for thatching.

The stooks are carried to and from the threshing field, piled on donkeys that one meets everywhere at this season, with their black, unbridled heads just visible beneath a pinnacle of golden straw.

While the threshing is going on sons and daughters keep turning up with one thing and another till there is a little crowd on the rocks, and any one who is passing stops for an hour or two to talk on his way to the sea, so that, like the kelp-burning in the summer-time, this work is full of sociability.

When the threshing is over the straw is taken up to the cottages and piled up in an outhouse, or more often in a corner of the kitchen, where it brings a new liveliness of colour.

A few days ago when I was visiting a cottage where there are the most beautiful children on the island, the eldest daughter, a girl of about fourteen, went and sat down on a heap of straw by the doorway. A ray of sunlight fell on her and on a portion of the rye, giving her figure and red dress with the straw under it a curious relief against the nets and oilskins, and forming a natural picture of exquisite harmony and colour.

In our own cottage the thatching – it is done every year – has just been carried out. The rope-twisting was done partly in the lane, partly in the kitchen when the weather was uncertain. Two men usually sit together at this work, one of them hammering the straw with a heavy block of wood, the other forming the rope, the main body of which is twisted by a boy or girl with a bent stick specially formed for this employment.

In wet weather, when the work must be done indoors, the person who is twisting recedes gradually out of the door, across the lane, and sometimes across a field or two beyond it. A great length is needed to form the close network which is spread over the thatch, as each piece measures about fifty yards. When this work is in progress in half of the cottages of the village, the road has a curious look, and one has to pick one's steps through a maze of twisting ropes that pass from the dark doorways on either side into the fields.

When four or five immense balls of rope have been completed, a thatching party is arranged, and before dawn some morning they come down to the house, and the work is taken in hand with such energy that it is usually ended within the day.

Like all work that is done in common on the island, the thatching is regarded as a sort of festival. From the moment a roof is taken in hand there is a whirl of laughter and talk till it is ended, and, as the man whose house is being covered is a host instead of an employer, he lays himself out to please the men who work with him.

The day our own house was thatched the large table was

taken into the kitchen from my room, and high teas were given every few hours. Most of the people who came along the road turned down into the kitchen for a few minutes, and the talking was incessant. Once when I went into the window I heard Michael retailing my astronomical lectures from the apex of the gable, but usually their topics have to do with the affairs of the island.

It is likely that much of the intelligence and charm of these people is due to the absence of any division of labour, and to the correspondingly wide development of each individual, whose varied knowledge and skill necessitate a considerable activity of mind. Each man can speak two languages. He is a skilled fisherman, and can manage a curagh with extraordinary nerve and dexterity. He can farm simply, burn kelp, cut out pampooties, mend nets, build and thatch a house, and make a cradle or a coffin. His work changes with the seasons in a way that keeps him free from the dullness that comes to people who have always the same occupation. The danger of his life on the sea gives him the alertness of a primitive hunter, and the long nights he spends fishing in his curagh bring him some of the emotions that are thought peculiar to men who have lived with the arts.

As Michael is busy in the daytime, I have got a boy to come up and read Irish to me every afternoon. He is about fifteen, and is singularly intelligent, with a real sympathy for the language and the stories we read.

One evening when he had been reading to me for two hours, I asked him if he was tired.

'Tired?' he said, 'sure you wouldn't ever be tired reading!'

A few years ago this predisposition for intellectual things would have made him sit with old people and learn their stories, but now boys like him turn to books and to papers in Irish that are sent them from Dublin.

In most of the stories we read, where the English and Irish are printed side by side, I see him looking across to the English in passages that are a little obscure, though he is indignant if I say that he knows English better than Irish. Probably he knows the local Irish better than English, and printed English better than printed Irish, as the latter has frequent dialectic forms he does not know.

A few days ago, when he was reading a folk-tale from Douglas Hyde's *Beside the Fire*, something caught his eye in the translation.

'There's a mistake in the English,' he said, after a moment's hesitation; 'he's put "gold chair" instead of "golden chair".'

I pointed out that we speak of gold watches and gold pins.

'And why wouldn't we?' he said; 'but "golden chair" would be much nicer.'

It is curious to see how his rudimentary culture has given him the beginning of a critical spirit that occupies itself with the form of language as well as with ideas.

One day I alluded to my trick of joining string.

'You can't join a string, don't be saying it,' he said; 'I don't know what way you're after fooling us, but you didn't join that string, not a bit of you.'

Another day when he was with me the fire burned low and I held up a newspaper before it to make a draught. It did not answer very well, and though the boy said nothing I saw he thought me a fool.

The next day he ran up in great excitement.

'I'm after trying the paper over the fire,' he said, 'and it burned grand. Didn't I think, when I seen you doing it there was no good in it at all, but I put a paper over the master's (the schoolmaster's) fire and it flamed up. Then I pulled back the corner of the paper and I ran my head in, and believe me, there was a big cold wind blowing up the chimney that would sweep the head from you.'

We nearly quarrelled because he wanted me to take his photograph in his Sunday clothes from Galway, instead of his native homespuns that become him far better, though he does not like them as they seem to connect him with the primitive life of the island. With his keen temperament, he may go far if he can ever step out into the world.

He is constantly thinking.

One day he asked me if there was great wonder on their names out in the country.

I said there was no wonder on them at all.

'Well,' he said, 'there is great wonder on your name in the island, and I was thinking maybe there would be great wonder on our names out in the country.'

In a sense he is right. Though the names here are ordinary enough, they are used in a way that differs altogether from the modern system of surnames.

When a child begins to wander about the island, the neighbours speak of it by its Christian name, followed by the Christian name of its father. If this is not enough to identify it, the father's epithet – whether it is a nickname or the name of his own father – is added.

Sometimes when the father's name does not lend itself, the mother's Christian name is adopted as epithet for the children.

An old woman near this cottage is called 'Peigín', and her sons are 'Peaits Pheigín', 'Seán Pheigín', etc.

Occasionally the surname is employed in its Irish form, but I have not heard them using the 'Mac' prefix when speaking Irish among themselves; perhaps the idea of a surname which it gives is too modern for them, perhaps they do use it at times that I have not noticed.

Sometimes a man is named from the colour of his hair. There is thus a Seán Rua (Red John), and his children are 'Máirtín Sheáin Rua', etc.

Another man is known as 'an t-iascaire' ('the fisher'), and his children are 'Máire an iascaire' ('Mary daughter of the fisher'), and so on.

The schoolmaster tells me that when he reads out the roll in the morning the children repeat the local name all together in a whisper after each official name, and then the child answers. If he calls, for instance, 'Patrick O'Flaherty', the children murmur, 'Peaits Sheáin Dheirg or some such name, and the boy answers.

People who come to the island are treated in much the same way. A French Gaelic student was in the islands recently, and he is always spoken of as 'An Sagart Rua' ('the red priest') or as 'An Sagart Francach' ('the French priest'), but never by his name.

If an islander's name alone is enough to distinguish him it is used by itself, and I know one man who is spoken of as Éamonn. There may be other Edmunds on the island, but if so they have probably good nicknames or epithets of their own.

In other countries where the names are in a somewhat similar condition, as in modern Greece, the man's calling is usually one of the most common means of distinguishing him, but in this place, where all have the same calling, this means is not available.

Late this evening I saw a three-oared curagh with two old women in her besides the rowers, landing at the slip through a heavy roll. They were coming from Inishere, and they rowed up quickly enough till they were within a few yards of the surf-line, where they spun round and waited with the prow towards the sea, while wave after wave passed underneath them and broke on the remains of the slip. Five minutes passed; ten minutes; and still they waited with the oars just paddling in the water, and their heads turned over their shoulders.

I was beginning to think that they would have to give up and row round to the lee side of the island, when the curagh seemed suddenly to turn into a living thing. The prow was again towards the slip, leaping and hurling itself through the spray. Before it touched, the man in the bow wheeled round, two white legs came out over the prow like the flash of a sword, and before the next wave arrived he had dragged the curagh out of danger.

This sudden and united action in men without discipline shows well the education that the waves have given them. When the curagh was in safety the two old women were carried up through the surf and slippery seaweed on the backs of their sons.

In this broken weather a curagh cannot go out without danger, yet accidents are rare and seem to be nearly always caused by drink. Since I was here last year four men have been drowned on their way home from the large island. First a curagh belonging to the south island which put off with two men in her heavy with drink, came to shore here the next evening dry and uninjured, with the sail half set, and no one in her.

More recently a curagh from this island with three men, who were the worse for drink, was upset on its way home. The steamer was not far off, and saved two of the men, but could not reach the third.

Now a man has been washed ashore in Donegal with one pampooty on him, and a striped shirt with a purse in one of the pockets, and a box for tobacco.

For three days the people here have been trying to fix his identity. Some think it is the man from this island, others think that the man from the south answers the description more exactly. Tonight as we were returning from the slip we met the mother of the man who was drowned from this island, still weeping and looking out over the sea. She stopped the people who had come over from the south island to ask them with a terrified whisper what is thought over there.

Later in the evening, when I was sitting in one of the cottages, the sister of the dead man came in through the rain with her infant, and there was a long talk about the rumours that had come in. She pieced together all she could remember about his clothes, and what his purse was like, and where he had got it, and the same for his tobacco box, and his stocking. In the end there seemed little doubt that it was her brother.

'Ah!' she said, 'it's Mike sure enough, and please God they'll give him a decent burial.'

Then she began to keen slowly to herself. She had loose yellow hair plastered round her head with the rain, and as she sat by the door suckling her infant, she seemed like a type of the women's life upon the islands.[39]

For a while the people sat silent, and one could hear nothing but the lips of the infant, the rain hissing in the yard, and the breathing of four pigs that lay sleeping in one corner. Then one of the men began to talk about the new boats that have been sent to the south island, and the conversation went back to its usual round of topics.

The loss of one man seems a slight catastrophe to all except the immediate relatives. Often when an accident happens a father is lost with his two eldest sons, or in some other way all the active men of a household die together.

A few years ago three men of a family that used to make the wooden vessels – like tiny barrels – that are still used among the people, went to the big island together. They were drowned on their way home, and the art of making these little barrels died with them, at least on Inishmaan, though it still lingers in the north and south islands.

Another catastrophe that took place last winter gave a curious zest to the observance of holy days. It seems that it is not the custom for the men to go out fishing on the evening of a holy day, but one night last December some men, who wished to begin fishing early the next morning, rowed out to sleep in their hookers.

Towards morning a terrible storm rose, and several hookers with their crews on board were blown from their moorings and wrecked. The sea was so high that no attempt at rescue could be made, and the men were drowned.

'Ah!' said the man who told me the story, 'I'm thinking it will be a long time before men will go out again on a holy day. That storm was the only storm that reached into the harbour the whole winter, and I'm thinking there was something in it.'[40]

Today when I went down to the slip I found a pig-jobber from Kilronan with about twenty pigs that were to be shipped for the English market.

When the steamer was getting near, the whole drove was moved down on the slip and the curaghs were carried out close to the sea. Then each beast was caught in its turn and thrown on its side, while its legs were hitched together in a single knot, with a tag of rope remaining, by which it could be carried.

Probably the pain inflicted was not great, yet the animals shut their eyes and shrieked with almost human intonations, till the suggestion of the noise became so intense that the men and women who were merely looking on grew wild with excitement, and the pigs waiting their turn foamed at the mouth and tore each other with their teeth.

After a while there was a pause. The whole slip was covered with a mass of sobbing animals, with here and there a terrified woman crouching among the bodies, and patting some special favourite to keep it quiet while the curaghs were being launched.

Then the screaming began again while the pigs were carried out and laid in their places, with a waistcoat tied round their feet to keep them from damaging the canvas. They seemed to know where they were going, and looked up at me over the gunnel with an ignoble desperation that made me shudder to think that I had eaten of this whimpering flesh. When the last curagh went out I was left on the slip with a band of women and children, and one old boar who sat looking out over the sea.

The women were over-excited, and when I tried to talk to them they crowded round me and began jeering and shrieking at me because I am not married. A dozen screamed at a time, and so rapidly that I could not understand all they were saying, yet I was able to make out that they were taking advantage of the absence of their husbands to give me the full volume of their contempt. Some little boys who were listening threw themselves down, writhing with laughter among the seaweed, and the young girls grew red with embarrassment and stared down into the surf.

For a moment I was in confusion. I tried to speak to them, but I could not make myself heard, so I sat down on the slip and drew out my wallet of photographs. In an instant I had the whole band clambering round me, in their ordinary mood.

When the curaghs came back – one of them towing a large kitchen table that stood itself up on the waves and then turned somersaults in an extraordinary manner – word went round that the ceannaí (pedlar) was arriving.

He opened his wares on the slip as soon as he landed, and sold a quantity of cheap knives and jewellery to the girls and younger women. He spoke no Irish, and the bargaining gave immense amusement to the crowd that collected round him.

I was surprised to notice that several women who professed to know no English could make themselves understood without difficulty when it pleased them.

'The rings is too dear at you, sir,' said one girl using the Gaelic construction; 'let you put less money on them and all the girls will be buying.'

After the jewellery he displayed some cheap religious pictures – abominable oleographs – but I did not see many buyers.

I am told that most of the pedlars who come here are Germans or Poles, but I did not have occasion to speak with this man by himself.

I have come over for a few days to the south island, and, as usual, my voyage was not favourable.

The morning was fine, and seemed to promise one of the peculiarly hushed, pellucid days that occur sometimes before rain in early winter. From the first gleam of dawn the sky was covered with white cloud, and the tranquillity was so complete that every sound seemed to float away by itself across the silence of the bay. Lines of blue smoke were going up in spirals over the village, and further off heavy fragments of rain-cloud were lying on the horizon. We started early in the day, and, although the sea looked calm from a distance, we met a considerable roll coming from the south-west when we got out from the shore.

Near the middle of the sound the man who was rowing in the bow broke his oar-pin, and the proper management of the canoe became a matter of some difficulty. We had only a three-oared curagh, and if the sea had gone much higher we should have run a good deal of danger. Our progress was so slow that clouds came up with a rise in the wind before we reached the shore, and rain began to fall in large single drops. The black curagh working slowly through this world of grey, and the soft hissing of the rain gave me one of the moods in which we realize with immense distress the short moment we have left us to experience all the wonder and beauty of the world.

The approach to the south island is made at a fine sandy beach on the north-west. This interval in the rocks is of great service to the people, but the tract of wet sand with a few hideous fishermen's houses, lately built on it, looks singularly desolate in broken weather.

The tide was going out when we landed, so we merely stranded the curagh and went up to the little hotel. The cess-collector[41] was at work in one of the rooms, and there were a number of men and boys waiting about, who stared at us while we stood at the door and talked to the proprietor.

When we had had our drink I went down to the sea with my men, who were in a hurry to be off. Some time was spent in replacing the oar-pin, and then they set out, though the wind was still increasing. A good many fishermen came down to see the start, and long after the curagh was out of sight I stood and talked with them in Irish, as I was anxious to compare their language and temperament with what I knew of the other island.

The language seems to be identical, though some of these men speak rather more distinctly than any Irish speakers I have yet heard. In physical type, dress, and general character, however, there seems to be a considerable difference. The people on this island are more advanced than their neighbours, and the families here are gradually forming into different ranks, made up of the well-to-do, the struggling, and the quite poor and thriftless. These distinctions are present in the middle island also, but over there they have had no effect on the people, among whom there is still absolute equality.

A little later the steamer came in sight and lay to in the offing. While the curaghs were being put out I noticed in the crowd several men of the ragged, humorous type that was once thought to represent the real peasant of Ireland. Rain was now falling heavily, and as we looked out through the fog there was something nearly appalling in the shrieks of laughter kept up by one of these individuals, a man of extraordinary ugliness and wit.

At last he moved off toward the houses, wiping his eyes with the tail of his coat and moaning to himself 'Tá mé marbh', ('I'm killed'), till some one stopped him and he began again pouring out a medley of rude puns and jokes that meant more than they said.

There is quaint humour, and sometimes wild humour, on the middle island, but never this half-sensual ecstasy of laughter. Perhaps a man must have a sense of intimate misery, not known there, before he can set himself to jeer and mock at the world. These strange men with receding foreheads, high cheek-bones, and ungovernable eyes seem to represent some old type found on these few acres at the extreme border of Europe, where it is only in wild jests and laughter that they can express their loneliness and desolation.

The mode of reciting ballads in this island is singularly harsh. I fell in with a curious man today beyond the east village, and we wandered out on the rocks towards the sea. A wintry shower came on while we were together, and we crouched down in the bracken, under a loose wall. When we had gone through the usual topics he asked me if I was fond of songs, and began singing to show what he could do.

The music was much like what I have heard before on the islands – a monotonous chant with pauses on the high and low notes to mark the rhythm; but the harsh nasal tone in which he sang was almost intolerable. His performance reminded me in general effect of a chant I once heard from a party of Orientals I was travelling with in a third-class carriage from Paris to Dieppe, but the islander ran his voice over a much wider range.

His pronunciation was lost in the rasping of his throat, and, though he shrieked into my ear to make sure that I understood him above the howling of the wind, I could only make out that it was an endless ballad telling the fortune of a young man who went to sea, and had many adventures. The English nautical terms were employed continually in describing his life on the ship, but the man seemed to feel that they were not in their place, and stopped short when one of them occurred to give me a poke with his finger and explain gib, topsail, and bowsprit, which were for me the most intelligible features of the poem. Again, when the scene changed to Dublin, 'glass of whisky', 'public-house', and such things were in English.

When the shower was over he showed me a curious cave hidden among the cliffs, a short distance from the sea. On our way back he asked me the three questions I am met with on every side – whether I am a rich man, whether I am married, and whether I have ever seen a poorer place than these islands.

When he heard that I was not married he urged me to come back in the summer so that he might take me over in a curagh to the Spa in County Clare, where there is 'spraoi mór agus go leor ladies' ('a big spree and plenty of ladies').[42]

Something about the man repelled me while I was with him, and though I was cordial and liberal he seemed to feel that I abhorred him. We arranged to meet again in the evening, but when I dragged myself with an inexplicable loathing to the place of meeting, there was no trace of him.

It is characteristic that this man, who is probably a drunkard and shebeener[43] and certainly in penury, refused the chance of a shilling because he felt that I did not like him. He had a curiously mixed expression of hardness and melancholy. Probably his character has given him a bad reputation on the island, and he lives here with the restlessness of a man who has no sympathy with his companions.

I have come over again to Inishmaan, and this time I had fine weather for my passage. The air was full of luminous sunshine from the early morning, and it was almost a summer's day when I set sail at noon with Michael and two other men who had come over for me in a curagh.

The wind was in our favour, so the sail was put up and Michael sat in the stern to steer with an oar while I rowed with the others.

We had had a good dinner and drink and were wrought up by this sudden revival of summer to a dreamy voluptuous gaiety, that made us shout with exultation to hear our voices passing out across the blue twinkling of the sea.

Even after the people of the south island, these men of the Inishmaan seemed to be moved by strange archaic sympathies with the world. Their mood accorded itself with wonderful fineness to the suggestions of the day, and their ancient Gaelic seemed so full of divine simplicity that I would have liked to turn the prow to the west and row with them for ever.

I told them I was going back to Paris in a few days to sell my books and my bed, and that then I was coming back to grow as strong and simple as they were among the islands of the west.

When our excitement sobered down, Michael told me that one of the priests had left his gun at our cottage and given me leave to use it till he returned to the island. There was another gun and a ferret in the house also, and he said that as soon as we got home he was going to take me out fowling on rabbits.

A little later in the day we set off, and I nearly laughed to see Michael's eagerness that I should turn out a good shot.

We put the ferret down in a crevice between two bare sheets of rock, and waited. In a few minutes we heard rushing paws underneath us, then a rabbit shot up straight into the air from the crevice at our feet and set off for a wall that was a few feet away. I threw up the gun and fired.

'Bhuail tú é,' screamed Michael at my elbow as he ran up the rock. I had killed it.

We shot seven or eight more in the next hour, and Michael was immensely pleased. If I had done badly I think I should have had to leave the islands. The people would have despised me. A 'duine uasal' who cannot shoot seems to these descendants of hunters a fallen type who is worse than an apostate.

The women of this island are before conventionality, and share some of the liberal features that are thought peculiar to the women of Paris and New York.

Many of them are too contented and too sturdy to have more than a decorative interest, but there are others full of curious individuality.

This year I have got to know a wonderfully humorous girl, who has been spinning in the kitchen for the last few days with the old woman's spinning-wheel. The morning she began I heard her exquisite intonation almost before I awoke, brooding and cooing over every syllable she uttered.

I have heard something similar in the voices of German and Polish women, but I do not think men – at least European men – who are always further than women from the simple, animal emotions, or any speakers who use languages with weak gutturals, like French or English, can produce this inarticulate chant in their ordinary talk.

She plays continual tricks with her Gaelic in the way girls are fond of, piling up diminutives and repeating adjectives with a humorous scorn of syntax. While she is here the talk never stops in the kitchen. Today she has been asking me many questions about Germany, for it seems one of her sisters married a German husband in America some years ago, who kept her in great comfort, with a fine 'capall glas' ('grey horse') to ride on, and this girl has decided to escape in the same way from the drudgery of the island.

This was my last evening on my stool in the chimney corner, and I had a long talk with some neighbours who came in to bid me prosperity, and lay about on the floor with their heads on low stools and their feet stretched out to the embers of the turf. The old woman was at the other side of the fire, and the girl I have spoken of was standing at her spinning-wheel, talking and joking with every one. She says when I go away now I am to marry a rich wife with plenty of money, and if she dies on me I am to come back here and marry herself for my second wife.

I have never heard talk so simple and so attractive as the talk of these people. This evening they began disputing about their wives, and it appeared that the greatest merit they see in a woman is that she should be fruitful and bring them many children. As no money can be earned by children on the island this one attitude shows the immense difference between these people and the people of Paris.

The direct sexual instincts are not weak on the island, but they are so subordinated to the instincts of the family that they rarely lead to irregularity. The life here is still at an almost patriarchal stage, and the people are nearly as far from the romantic moods of love as they are from the impulsive life of the savage.

The wind was so high this morning that there was some doubt whether the steamer would arrive, and I spent half the day wandering about with Michael watching the horizon.

At last, when we had given her up, she came in sight far away to the north, where she had gone to have the wind with her where the sea was at its highest.

I got my baggage from the cottage and set off for the slip with Michael and the old man, turning into a cottage here and there to say goodbye.

In spite of the wind outside, the sea at the slip was as calm as a pool. The men who were standing about while the steamer was at the south island wondered for the last time whether I would be married when I came back to see them. Then we pulled out and took our place in the line. As the tide was running hard the steamer stopped a certain distance from the shore, and gave us a long race for good places at her side. In the struggle we did not come off well, so I had to clamber across two curaghs, twisting and fumbling with the roll, in order to get on board.

It seemed strange to see the curaghs full of well-known faces turning back to the slip without me, but the roll in the sound soon took off my attention. Some men were on board whom I had seen on the south island, and a good many Kilronan people on their way home from Galway, who told me that in one part of their passage in the morning they had come in for heavy seas.

As is usual on Saturday, the steamer had a large cargo of flour and porter to discharge at Kilronan, and, as it was nearly four o'clock before the tide could float her at the pier, I felt some doubt about our passage to Galway.

The wind increased as the afternoon went on, and when I came down in the twilight I found that the cargo was not yet all unladen, and that the captain feared to face the gale that was rising. It was some time before he came to a final decision, and we walked backwards and forwards from the village with heavy clouds flying overhead and the wind howling in the walls. At last he telegraphed to Galway to know if he was wanted the next day, and we went into a public-house to wait for the reply.

The kitchen was filled with men sitting closely on long forms ranged in lines at each side of the fire. A wild-looking but beautiful girl was kneeling on the hearth talking loudly to the men, and a few natives of Inishmaan were hanging about the door, miserably drunk. At the end of the kitchen the bar was arranged, with a sort of alcove beside it, where some older men were playing cards. Overhead there were the open rafters, filled with turf and tobacco smoke.

This is the haunt so much dreaded by the women of the other islands, where the men linger with their money till they go out at last with reeling steps and are lost in the sound. Without this background of empty curaghs, and bodies floating naked with the tide, there would be something almost absurd about the dissipation of this simple place where men sit, evening after evening, drinking bad whisky and porter, and talking with endless repetition of fishing, and kelp, and of the sorrows of purgatory.

When we had finished our whisky word came that the boat might remain.

With some difficulty I got my bags out of the steamer and carried them up through the crowd of women and donkeys that were still struggling on the quay in an inconceivable medley of flour-bags and cases of petroleum. When I reached the inn the old woman was in great good humour, and I spent some time talking by the kitchen fire. Then I groped my way back to the harbour, where, I was told, the old net-mender, who came to see me on my first visit to the islands, was spending the night as watchman.

It was quite dark on the pier, and a terrible gale was blowing. There was no one in the little office where I expected to find him, so I groped my way further on towards a figure I saw moving with a lantern.

It was the old man, and he remembered me at once when I hailed him and told him who I was. He spent some time arranging one of his lanterns, and then he took me back to his office – a mere shed of planks and corrugated iron, put up for the contractor of some work which is in progress on the pier.

When we reached the light I saw that his head was rolled up in an extraordinary collection of mufflers to keep him from the cold, and that his face was much older than when I saw him before, though still full of intelligence.

He began to tell how he had gone to see a relative of mine[44] in Dublin when he first left the island as a cabin-boy, between forty and fifty years ago.

He told his story with the usual detail:

We saw a man walking about on the quay in Dublin, and looking at us without saying a word. Then he came down to the yacht.

'Are you the men from Aran?' said he.

'We are,' said we.

'You're to come with me so,' said he.

'Why?' said we.

Then he told us it was Mr Synge had sent him and we went with him. Mr Synge brought us into his kitchen and gave the men a glass of whisky all round, and a half-glass to me because I was a boy – though at that time and to this day I can drink as much as two men and not be the worse of it. We were some time in the kitchen, then one of the men said we should be going. I said it would not be right to go without saying a word to Mr Synge. Then the servant-girl went up and brought him down, and he gave us another glass of whisky, and he gave me a book in Irish because I was going to sea, and I was able to read in the Irish.

I owe it to Mr Synge and that book that when I came back here, after not hearing a word of Irish for thirty years, I had as good Irish, or maybe better Irish, than any person on the island.

I could see all through his talk that the sense of superiority which his scholarship in this little-known language gave him above the ordinary seaman, had influenced his whole personality and been the central interest of his life.

On one voyage he had a fellow-sailor who often boasted that he had been at school and learned Greek, and this incident took place:

One night we had a quarrel, and I asked him could he read a Greek book with all his talk of it.

'I can so,' said he.

'We'll see that,' said I.

Then I got the Irish book out of my chest, and I gave it into his hand.

'Read that to me,' said I, 'if you know Greek.'

He took it, and he looked at it this way, and that way, and not a bit of him could make it out.

'Bedad, I've forgotten my Greek,' said he.

'You're telling a lie,' said I.

'I'm not,' said he; 'it's the divil a bit I can read it.'

Then I took the book back into my hand, and said to him –

'It's the sorra a word of Greek you ever knew in your life, for there's not a word of Greek in that book, and not a bit of you knew.'

He told me another story of the only time he had heard Irish spoken during his voyages:

One night I was in New York, walking in the streets with some other men, and we came upon two women quarrelling in Irish at the door of a public-house.

'What's that jargon?' said one of the men.

'It's no jargon,' said I.

'What is it?' said he.

'It's Irish,' said I.

Then I went up to them, and you know, sir, there is no language like the Irish for soothing and quieting. The moment I spoke to them they stopped scratching and swearing and stood there as quiet as two lambs.

Then they asked me in Irish if I wouldn't come in and have a drink, and I said I couldn't leave my mates.

'Bring them too,' said they.

Then we all had a drop together.

While we were talking another man had slipped in and sat down in the corner with his pipe, and the rain had become so heavy we could hardly hear our voices over the noise on the iron roof.

The old man went on telling of his experiences at sea and the places he had been to.

'If I had my life to live over again,' he said, 'there's no other way I'd spend it. I went in and out everywhere and saw everything. I was never afraid to take my glass, though I was never drunk in my life, and I was a great player of cards though I never played for money.'

'There's no diversion at all in cards if you don't play for money,' said the man in the corner.

'There was no use in my playing for money,' said the old man, 'for I'd always lose, and what's the use in playing if you always lose?'

Then our conversation branched off to the Irish language and the books written in it.

He began to criticize Archbishop MacHale's version of *Moore's Irish Melodies*[45] with great severity and acuteness, citing whole poems both in the English and Irish, and then giving versions that he had made himself.

'A translation is no translation,' he said, 'unless it will give you the music of a poem along with the words of it. In my translation you won't find a foot or a syllable that's not in the English, yet I've put down all his words mean, and nothing but it. Archbishop MacHale's work is a most miserable production.'

From the verses he cited his judgement seemed perfectly justified, and even if he was wrong, it is interesting to note that this poor sailor and night-watchman was ready to rise up and criticize an eminent dignitary and scholar on rather delicate points of versification and the finer distinctions between old words of Gaelic.

In spite of his singular intelligence and minute observation his reasoning was medieval.

I asked him what he thought about the future of the language on these islands.

'It can never die out,' said he, 'because there's no family in the place can live without a bit of a field for potatoes, and they have only the Irish words for all that they do in the fields. They sail their new boats – their hookers – in English, but they sail a curagh oftener in Irish, and in the fields they have the Irish alone. It can never die out, and when the people begin to see it fallen very low, it will rise up again like the phoenix from its own ashes.'

'And the Gaelic League?' I asked him.

'The Gaelic League! Didn't they come down here with their organizers and their secretaries, and their meetings and their speechifyings, and start a branch of it, and teach a power of Irish for five weeks and a half!'*

'What do we want here with their teaching Irish?' said the man in the corner; 'haven't we Irish enough?'

'You have not,' said the old man; 'there's not a soul in Aran can count up to nine hundred and ninety-nine without using an English word but myself.'

It was getting late, and the rain had lessened for a moment, so I groped my way back to the inn through the intense darkness of a late autumn night.

---

* This was written, it should be remembered, some years ago.

PART IV

No two journeys to these islands are alike. This morning I
sailed with the steamer a little after five o'clock in a cold night
air, with the stars shining on the bay. A number of Claddagh
fishermen had been out all night fishing not far from the
harbour, and without thinking, or perhaps caring to think, of
the steamer, they had put out their nets in the channel where
she was to pass. Just before we started the mate sounded the
steam whistle repeatedly to give them warning, saying as he
did so –

'If you were out now in the bay, gentlemen, you'd hear some
fine prayers being said.'

When we had gone a little way we began to see the light from
the turf fires carried by the fishermen flickering on the water,
and to hear a faint noise of angry voices. Then the outline of a
large fishing-boat came in sight through the darkness, with the
forms of three men who stood on the deck shrieking and howling
at us to alter our course. The captain feared to turn aside, as
there are sandbanks near the channel, so the engines were
stopped and we glided over the nets without doing them harm.
As we passed close to the boat the crew could be seen plainly on
the deck, one of them holding the bucket of red turf, and their
abuse could be distinctly heard. It changed continually, from
profuse Gaelic maledictions to the simpler curses they know in
English. As they spoke they could be seen writhing and twisting
themselves with passion against the light which was beginning
to turn on the ripple of the sea. Soon afterwards another set of
voices began in front of us, breaking out in strange contrast
with the dwindling stars and the silence of the dawn.

Further on we passed many boats that let us go by without a
word, as their nets were not in the channel. Then day came on
rapidly with cold showers that turned golden in the first rays
from the sun, filling the troughs of the sea with curious trans-
parencies and light.

This year I have brought my fiddle with me so that I may have something new to keep up the interest of the people. I have played for them several tunes, but as far as I can judge they do not feel modern music, though they listen eagerly from curiosity. Irish airs like 'Eileen Aroon' please them better, but it is only when I play some jig like the 'Black Rogue' – which is known on the island – that they seem to respond to the full meaning of the notes. Last night I played for a large crowd, which had come together for another purpose from all parts of the island.

About six o'clock I was going into the schoolmaster's house, and I heard a fierce wrangle going on between a man and a woman near the cottages to the west, that lie below the road. While I was listening to them several women came down to listen also from behind the wall, and told me that the people who were fighting were near relations who lived side by side and often quarrelled about trifles, though they were as good friends as ever the next day. The voices sounded so enraged that I thought mischief would come of it, but the women laughed at the idea. Then a lull came, and I said that they seemed to have finished at last.

'Finished!' said one of the women; 'sure they haven't rightly begun. It's only playing they are yet.'

It was just after sunset and the evening was bitterly cold, so I went into the house and left them.

An hour later the old man came down from my cottage to say that some of the lads and the 'fear líonta' ('the man of the nets' – a young man from Aranmor who is teaching net-mending to the boys) were up at the house, and had sent him down to tell me they would like to dance, if I would come up and play for them.

I went out at once, and as soon as I came into the air I heard the dispute going on still to the west more violently than ever. The news of it had gone about the island, and little bands of girls and boys were running along the lanes towards the scene of the quarrel as eagerly as if they were going to a racecourse.

I stopped for a few minutes at the door of our cottage to listen to the volume of abuse that was rising across the stillness of the island. Then I went into the kitchen and began tuning the fiddle, as the boys were impatient for my music. At first I tried to play standing, but on the upward stroke my bow came in contact with the salt-fish and oilskins that hung from the rafters, so I settled myself at last on a table in the corner, where I was out of the way, and got one of the people to hold up my music before me, as I had no stand. I played a French melody first, to get myself used to the people and the qualities of the room, which has little resonance between the earth floor and the thatch overhead. Then I struck up the 'Black Rogue', and in a moment a tall man bounded out from his stool under the chimney and began flying round the kitchen with peculiarly sure and graceful bravado.

The lightness of the pampooties seems to make the dancing on this island lighter and swifter than anything I have seen on the mainland, and the simplicity of the men enables them to throw a naïve extravagance into their steps that is impossible in places where the people are self-conscious.

The speed, however, was so violent that I had some difficulty in keeping up, as my fingers were not in practice, and I could not take off more than a small part of my attention to watch what was going on. When I finished I heard a commotion at the door, and the whole body of people who had gone down to watch the quarrel filed into the kitchen and arranged themselves around the walls, the women and girls, as is usual, forming themselves in one compact mass crouching on their heels near the door.

I struck up another dance – 'Paddy Get Up' – and the 'fear líonta' and the first dancer went through it together, with additional rapidity and grace, as they were excited by the presence of the people who had come in. Then word went round that an old man, known as Little Roger, was outside, and they told me he was once the best dancer on the island.

For a long time he refused to come in, for he said he was too old to dance, but at last he was persuaded, and the people brought him in and gave him a stool opposite me. It was some time longer before he would take his turn, and when he did so, though he was met with great clapping of hands, he only danced for a few moments. He did not know the dances in my book, he said, and did not care to dance to music he was not familiar with. When the people pressed him again he looked across to me.

'John,' he said, in shaking English, 'have you got "Larry Grogan", for it is an agreeable air?'

I had not, so some of the young men danced again to the 'Black Rogue', and then the party broke up. The altercation was still going on at the cottage below us, and the people were anxious to see what was coming of it.

About ten o'clock a young man came in and told us that the fight was over.

'They have been at it for four hours,' he said, 'and now they're tired. Indeed it is time they were, for you'd rather be listening to a man killing a pig than to the noise they were letting out of them.'

After the dancing and excitement we were too stirred up to be sleepy, so we sat for a long time round the embers of the turf, talking and smoking by the light of a candle.

From ordinary music we came to talk of the music of the fairies, and they told me this story, when I had told them some stories of my own:

A man who lives in the other end of the village got his gun one day and went out to look for rabbits in a thicket near the small Dun. He saw a rabbit sitting up under a tree, and he lifted his gun to take aim at it, but just as he had it covered he heard a kind of music over his head, and he looked up into the sky. When he looked back for the rabbit, not a bit of it was to be seen.

He went on after that, and he heard the music again.

Then he looked over a wall, and he saw a rabbit sitting up by the wall with a sort of flute in its mouth, and it playing on it with its two fingers!

'What sort of a rabbit was that?' said the old woman when they had finished. 'How could that be a right rabbit? I remember old Pat Dirane used to be telling us he was once out on the cliffs, and he saw a big rabbit sitting down in a hole under a flagstone. He called a man who was with him, and they put a hook on the end of a stick and ran it down into the hole. Then a voice called up to them –

'"Ah, a Phádraic, don't hurt me with the hook!"'

'Pat was a great rogue,' said the old man. 'Maybe you remember the bits of horns he had like handles on the end of his sticks? Well, one day there was a priest over and he said to Pat –

'"Is it the devil's horns you have on your sticks, Pat?"

'"I don't rightly know," said Pat, "but if it is, it's the devil's milk you've been drinking, since you've been able to drink, and the devil's flesh you've been eating and the devil's butter you've been putting on your bread, for I've seen the like of them horns on every old cow through the country."'

The weather has been rough, but early this afternoon the sea was calm enough for a hooker to come in with turf from Connemara, though while she was at the pier the roll was so great that the men had to keep a watch on the waves and loosen the cable whenever a large one was coming in, so that she might ease up with the water.

There were only two men on board, and when she was empty they had some trouble in dragging in the cables, hoisting the sails, and getting out of the harbour before they could be blown on the rocks.

A heavy shower came on soon afterwards, and I lay down under a stack of turf with some people who were standing about, to wait for another hooker that was coming in with horses. They began talking and laughing about the dispute last night and the noise made at it.

'The worst fights do be made here over nothing,' said an old man next me. 'Did Máirtín or any of them on the big island ever tell you of the fight they had there threescore years ago when they were killing each other with knives out on the strand?'

'They never told me,' I said.

'Well,' said he, 'they were going down to cut weed, and a

man was sharpening his knife on a stone before he went. A young boy came into the kitchen, and he said to the man –

'"What are you sharpening that knife for?"

'"To kill your father with," said the man, and they the best of friends all the time. The young boy went back to his house and told his father there was a man sharpening a knife to kill him.

'"Bedad," said the father, "if he has a knife I'll have one too."

'He sharpened his knife after that, and they went down to the strand. Then the two men began making fun about their knives, and from that they began raising their voices, and it wasn't long before there were ten men fighting with their knives, and they never stopped till there were five of them dead.

'They buried them the day after, and when they were coming home, what did they see but the boy who began the work playing about with the son of the other man, and their two fathers down in their graves.'

When he stopped, a gust of wind came and blew up a bundle of dry seaweed that was near us, right over our heads.

Another old man began to talk.

'That was a great wind,' he said. 'I remember one time there was a man in the south island who had a lot of wool up in shelter against the corner of a wall. He was after washing it, and drying it, and turning it, and he had it all nice and clean the way they could card it. Then a wind came down and the wool began blowing all over the wall. The man was throwing out his arms on it and trying to stop it, and another man saw him.

'"The devil mend your head!" says he, "the like of that wind is too strong for you."

'"If the devil himself is in it," said the other man, "I'll hold on to it while I can."

'Then whether it was because of the word or not I don't know, but the whole of the wool went up over his head and blew all over the island, yet, when his wife came to spin afterwards she had all they expected, as if that lot was not lost on them at all.'

'There was more than that in it,' said another man, 'for the night before a woman had a great sight out to the west in this island, and saw all the people that were dead a while back in this island and the south island, and they all talking with each other. There was a man over from the other island that night, and he heard the woman talking of what she had seen. The next day he went back to the south island, and I think he was alone in the curagh. As soon as he came near the other island he saw a man fishing from the cliffs, and this man called out to him –

'"Make haste now and go up and tell your mother to hide the poteen" – his mother used to sell poteen – "for I'm after seeing the biggest party of peelers and yeomanry passing by on the rocks was ever seen on the island." It was at that time the wool was taken with the other man above, under the hill, and no peelers in the island at all.'

A little after that the old men went away, and I was left with some young men between twenty and thirty, who talked to me of different things. One of them asked me if ever I was drunk, and another told me I would be right to marry a girl out of this island, for they were nice women in it, fine fat girls, who would be strong, and have plenty of children, and not be wasting my money on me.

When the horses were coming ashore a curagh that was far out after lobster-pots came hurrying in, and a man out of her ran up the sandhills to meet a little girl who was coming down with a bundle of Sunday clothes. He changed them on the sand and then went out to the hooker, and went off to Connemara to bring back his horses.

A young married woman I used often to talk with is dying of a fever – typhus I am told – and her husband and brothers have gone off in a curagh to get the doctor and the priest from the north island, though the sea is rough.

I watched them from the Dun for a long time after they had started. Wind and rain were driving through the sound, and I could see no boats or people anywhere except this one black curagh splashing and struggling through the waves. When the wind fell a little I could hear people hammering below me to the east. The body of a young man who was drowned a few weeks ago came ashore this morning, and his friends have been busy all day making a coffin in the yard of the house where he lived.

After a while the curagh went out of sight into the mist, and I came down to the cottage shuddering with cold and misery.

The old woman was keening by the fire.

'I have been to the house where the young man is,' she said; 'but I couldn't go to the door with the air was coming out of it. They say his head isn't on him at all, and indeed it isn't any wonder and he three weeks in the sea. Isn't it great danger and sorrow is over every one on this island?'

I asked her if the curagh would soon be coming back with the priest.

'It will not be coming soon or at all tonight,' she said. 'The wind has gone up now, and there will come no curagh to this island for maybe two days or three. And wasn't it a cruel thing to see the haste was on them, and they in danger all the time to be drowned themselves?'

Then I asked her how the woman was doing.

'She's nearly lost,' said the old woman; 'she won't be alive at all tomorrow morning. They have no boards to make her a coffin, and they'll want to borrow the boards that a man below has had this two years to bury his mother, and she alive still. I heard them saying there are two more women with the fever, and a child that's not three. The Lord have mercy on us all!'

I went out again to look over the sea, but night had fallen and the hurricane was howling over the Dun. I walked down the lane and heard the keening in the house where the young man was. Further on I could see a stir about the door of the cottage that had been last struck by typhus. Then I turned back again in the teeth of the rain, and sat over the fire with the old man and woman talking of the sorrows of the people till it was late in the night.

This evening the old man told me a story he had heard long ago on the mainland:

There was a young woman, he said, and she had a child. In a little time the woman died and they buried her the day after. That night another woman – a woman of the family – was sitting by the fire with the child on her lap, giving milk to it out of a cup. Then the woman they were after burying opened the door, and came into the house. She went over to the fire, and she took a stool and sat down before the other woman. Then she put out her hand and took the child on her lap, and gave it her breast. After that she put the child in the cradle and went over to the dresser and took milk and potatoes off it, and ate them. Then she went out. The other woman was frightened, and she told the man of the house when he came back, and two young men. They said they would be there the next night, and if she came back they would catch hold of her. She came the next night and gave the child her breast, and when she got up to go to the dresser, the man of the house caught hold of her, but he fell down on the floor. Then the two young men caught hold of her and they held her. She told them she was away with the fairies, and they could not keep her that night, though she was eating no food with the fairies, the way she might be able to come back to her child. Then she told them they would all be leaving that part of the country on the Oíche Shamhna, and that there would be four or five hundred of them riding on horses, and herself would be on a grey horse, riding behind a young man. And she told them to go down to a bridge they would be crossing that night, and to wait at the head of it, and when she would be coming up she would slow the horse and they would be able to throw something on her and on the young man, and they would fall over on the ground and be saved.

She went away then, and on the Oíche Shamhna the men went down and got her back. She had four children after that, and in the end she died.

It was not herself they buried at all the first time, but some old thing the fairies put in her place.[46]

'There are people who say they don't believe in these things,' said the old woman, 'but there are strange things, let them say what they will. There was a woman went to bed at the lower village a while ago, and her child along with her. For a time they did not sleep, and then something came to the window, and they heard a voice and this is what it said –

' "It is time to sleep from this out."

'In the morning the child was dead, and indeed it is many get their death that way on the island.'

The young man has been buried, and his funeral was one of the strangest scenes I have met with. People could be seen going down to his house from early in the day, yet when I went there with the old man about the middle of the afternoon, the coffin was still lying in front of the door, with the men and women of the family standing round beating it, and keening over it, in a great crowd of people. A little later every one knelt down and a last prayer was said. Then the cousins of the dead man got ready two oars and some pieces of rope – the men of his own family seemed too broken with grief to know what they were doing – the coffin was tied up, and the procession began. The old women walked close behind the coffin, and I happened to take a place just after them, among the first of the men. The rough lane to the graveyard slopes away towards the east, and the crowd of women going down before me in their red dresses, cloaked with red petticoats, with the waistband that is held round the head just seen from behind, had a strange effect, to which the white coffin and the unity of colour gave a nearly cloistral quietness.

This time the graveyard was filled with withered grass and bracken instead of the early ferns that were to be seen everywhere at the other funeral I have spoken of, and the grief of the people was of a different kind, as they had come to bury a young man who had died in his first manhood, instead of an old woman of eighty. For this reason the keen lost a part of its formal nature, and was recited as the expression of intense personal grief by the young men and women of the man's own family.

When the coffin had been laid down, near the grave that was to be opened, two long switches were cut out from the brambles among the rocks, and the length and breadth of the coffin were marked on them. Then the men began their work, clearing off stones and thin layers of earth, and breaking up an old coffin that was in the place into which the new one had to be lowered. When a number of blackened boards and pieces of bone had been thrown up with the clay, a skull was lifted out, and placed upon a gravestone. Immediately the old woman, the mother of the dead man, took it up in her hands, and carried it away by herself. Then she sat down and put it in her lap – it was the skull of her own mother – and began keening and shrieking over it with the wildest lamentation.

As the pile of mouldering clay got higher beside the grave a heavy smell began to rise from it, and the men hurried with their work, measuring the hole repeatedly with the two rods of bramble. When it was nearly deep enough the old woman got up and came back to the coffin, and began to beat on it, holding the skull in her left hand. This last moment of grief was the most terrible of all. The young women were nearly lying among the stones, worn out with their passion of grief, yet raising themselves every few moments to beat with magnificent gestures on the boards of the coffin. The young men were worn out also, and their voices cracked continually in the wail of the keen.

When everything was ready the sheet was unpinned from the coffin, and it was lowered into its place. Then an old man took a wooden vessel with holy water in it, and a wisp of bracken, and the people crowded round him while he splashed the water over them. They seemed eager to get as much of it as possible, more than one old woman crying out with a humorous voice –

'Tabhair dhom braon eile, a Mháirtín.' ('Give me another drop, Martin.')

When the grave was half filled in, I wandered round towards the north watching two seals that were chasing each other near the surf. I reached the Sandy Head as the light began to fail, and found some of the men I knew best fishing there with a sort of drag-net. It is a tedious process, and I sat for a long time on the sand watching the net being put out, and then drawn in again by eight men working together with a slow rhythmical movement.

As they talked to me and gave me a little poteen and a little bread when they thought I was hungry, I could not help feeling that I was talking with men who were under a judgement of death. I knew that every one of them would be drowned in the sea in a few years and battered naked on the rocks, or would die in his own cottage and be buried with another fearful scene in the graveyard I had come from.

When I got up this morning I found that the people had gone to Mass and latched the kitchen door from the outside, so that I could not open it to give myself light.

I sat for nearly an hour beside the fire with a curious feeling that I should be quite alone in this little cottage. I am so used to sitting here with the people that I have never felt the room before as a place where any man might live and work by himself. After a while as I waited, with just light enough from the chimney to let me see the rafters and the greyness of the walls, I became indescribably mournful, for I felt that this little corner on the face of the world, and the people who live in it, have a peace and dignity from which we are shut for ever.

While I was dreaming, the old woman came in in a great hurry and made tea for me and the young priest, who followed her a little later drenched with rain and spray.

The curate who has charge of the middle and south islands has a wearisome and dangerous task. He comes to this island or Inishere on Saturday night – whenever the sea is calm enough – and has Mass the first thing on Sunday morning. Then he goes down fasting and is rowed across to the other island and has Mass again, so that it is about midday when he gets a hurried breakfast before he sets off again for Aranmor, meeting often on both passages a rough and perilous sea.

A couple of Sundays ago I was lying outside the cottage in the sunshine smoking my pipe, when the curate, a man of the greatest kindliness and humour, came up, wet and worn out, to have his first meal. He looked at me for a moment and then shook his head.

'Tell me,' he said, 'did you read your Bible this morning?'

I answered that I had not done so.

'Well, begob, Mr Synge,' he went on, 'if you ever go to Heaven, you'll have a great laugh at us.'

Although these people are kindly towards each other and to their children, they have no feeling for the sufferings of animals, and little sympathy for pain when the person who feels it is not in danger. I have sometimes seen a girl writhing and howling with toothache while her mother sat at the other side of the fireplace pointing at her and laughing at her as if amused by the sight.

A few days ago, when we had been talking of the death of President M'Kinley, I explained the American way of killing murderers, and a man asked me how long the man who killed the President would be dying.

'While you'd be snapping your fingers,' I said.

'Well,' said the man, 'they might as well hang him so, and not be bothering themselves with all them wires. A man who would kill a King or a President knows he has to die for it, and it's only giving him the thing he bargained for if he dies easy. It would be right he should be three weeks dying, and there'd be fewer of those things done in the world.'

If two dogs fight at the slip when we are waiting for the steamer, the men are delighted and do all they can to keep up the fury of the battle.

They tie down donkeys' heads to their hoofs to keep them from straying, in a way that must cause horrible pain, and sometimes when I go into a cottage I find all the women of the place down on their knees plucking the feathers from live ducks and geese.

When the people are in pain themselves they make no attempt to hide or control their feelings. An old man who was ill in the winter took me out the other day to show me how far down the road they could hear him yelling 'the time he had a pain in his head'.

There was a great storm this morning, and I went up on the

cliff to sit in the shanty they have made there for the men who watch for wrack.[47] Soon afterwards a boy, who was out minding sheep, came up from the west, and we had a long talk.

He began by giving me the first connected account I have had of the accident that happened some time ago, when the young man was drowned on his way to the south island.

'Some men from the south island,' he said, 'came over and bought some horses on this island, and they put them in a hooker to take across. They wanted a curagh to go with them to tow the horses on to the strand, and a young man said he would go, and they could give him a rope and tow him behind the hooker. When they were out in the sound a wind came down on them, and the man in the curagh couldn't turn her to meet the waves, because the hooker was pulling her and she began filling up with water.

'When the men in the hooker saw it they began crying out one thing and another thing without knowing what to do. One man called out to the man who was holding the rope: "Let go the rope now, or you'll swamp her."

'And the man with the rope threw it out on the water, and the curagh half-filled already, and I think only one oar in her. A wave came into her then, and she went down before them, and the young man began swimming about; then they let fall the sails in the hooker the way they could pick him up. And when they had them down they were too far off, and they pulled the sails up again the way they could tack back to him. He was there in the water swimming round, and swimming round, and before they got up with him again he sank the third time, and they didn't see any more of him.'

I asked if any one had seen him on the island since he was dead.

'They have not,' he said, 'but there were queer things in it. Before he went out on the sea that day his dog came up and sat beside him on the rocks, and began crying. When the horses were coming down to the slip an old woman saw her son, that was drowned a while ago, riding on one of them. She didn't say what she was after seeing, and this man caught the horse, he caught his own horse first, and then he caught this one, and after that he went out and was drowned. Two days after I dreamed they found him on the Ceann Gainimh (the Sandy Head) and carried him up to the house on the plain, and took his pampooties off him and hung them up on a nail to dry. It was there they found him afterwards as you'll have heard them say.'

'Are you always afraid when you hear a dog crying?' I said.

'We don't like it,' he answered; 'you will often see them on the top of the rocks looking up into the heavens, and they crying. We don't like it at all, and we don't like a cock or hen to break anything in a house, for we know then some one will be going away. A while before the man who used to live in that cottage below died in the winter, the cock belonging to his wife began to fight with another cock. The two of them flew up on the dresser and knocked the glass of the lamp off it, and it fell on the floor and was broken. The woman caught her cock after that and killed it, but she could not kill the other cock, for it was belonging to the man who lived in the next house. Then himself got a sickness and died after that.'

I asked if he ever heard the fairy music on the island.

'I heard some of the boys talking in the school a while ago,' he said, 'and they were saying that their brothers and another man went out fishing a morning, two weeks ago, before the cock crew. When they were down near the Sandy Head they heard music near them, and it was the fairies were in it. I've heard of other things too. One time three men were out at night in a curagh, and they saw a big ship coming down on them. They were frightened at it, and they tried to get away, but it came on nearer them, till one of the men turned round and made the sign of the cross, and then they didn't see it any more.'

Then he went on in answer to another question:

'We do often see the people who do be away with them. There was a young man died a year ago, and he used to come to the window of the house where his brothers slept, and be talking to them in the night. He was married a while before that, and he used to be saying in the night he was sorry he had not promised the land to his son, and that it was to him it should go. Another time he was saying something about a mare, about her hoofs, or the shoes they should put on her. A little while ago Peaits Rua saw him going down the road with bróga arda (leather boots) on him and a new suit. Then two men saw him in another place.

'Do you see that straight wall of cliff?' he went on a few moments later, pointing to a place below us. 'It is there the fairies do be playing ball in the night, and you can see the marks of their heels when you come in the morning, and three stones they have to mark the line, and another big stone they hop the ball on. It's often the boys have put away the three stones, and they will always be back again in the morning, and a while since the man who owns the land took the big stone itself and rolled it down and threw it over the cliff, yet in the morning it was back in its place before him.'

I am in the south island again, and I have come upon some old men with a wonderful variety of stories and songs, the last, fairly often, both in English and Irish. I went round to the house of one of them today, with a native scholar who can write Irish, and we took down a certain number, and heard others. Here is one of the tales the old man told us at first before he had warmed to his subject. I did not take it down, but it ran in this way:

There was a man of the name of Charley Lambert, and every horse he would ride in a race he would come in the first.

The people in the country were angry with him at last, and this law was made, that he should ride no more at races, and if he rode, any one who saw him would have the right to shoot him. After that there was a gentleman from that part of the country over in England, and he was talking one day with the people there, and he said that the horses of Ireland were the best horses. The English said it was the English horses were the best, and at last they said there should be a race, and the English horses would come over and race against the horses of Ireland, and the gentleman put all his money on that race.

Well, when he came back to Ireland he went to Charley

Lambert, and asked him to ride on his horse. Charley said he would not ride, and told the gentleman the danger he'd be in. Then the gentleman told him the way he had put all his property on the horse, and at last Charley asked where the races were to be, and the hour and the day. The gentleman told him.

'Let you put a horse with a bridle and saddle on it every seven miles along the road from here to the racecourse on that day,' said Lambert, 'and I'll be in it.'

When the gentleman was gone, Charley stripped off his clothes and got into his bed. Then he sent for the doctor, and when he heard him coming he began throwing about his arms the way the doctor would think his pulse was up with the fever.

The doctor felt his pulse and told him to stay quiet till the next day, when he would see him again.

The next day it was the same thing, and so on till the day of the races. That morning Charley had his pulse beating so hard the doctor thought bad of him.

'I'm going to the races now, Charley,' said he, 'but I'll come in and see you again when I'll be coming back in the evening, and let you be very careful and quiet till you see me.'

As soon as he had gone Charley leapt up out of bed and got on his horse, and rode seven miles to where the first horse was waiting for him. Then he rode that horse seven miles, and another horse seven miles more, till he came to the racecourse.

He rode on the gentleman's horse, and he won the race.

There were great crowds looking on, and when they saw him coming in they said it was Charley Lambert, or the devil was in it, for there was no one else could bring in a horse the way he did, for the leg was after being knocked off of the horse and he came in all the same.

When the race was over, he got up on the horse was waiting for him, and away with him for seven miles. Then he rode the other horse seven miles, and his own horse seven miles, and when he got home he threw off his clothes and lay down on his bed.

After a while the doctor came back and said it was a great race they were after having.

The next day the people were saying it was Charley Lambert was the man who rode the horse. An inquiry was held, and the doctor swore that Charley was ill in his bed, and he had seen him before the race and after it, so the gentleman saved his fortune.[48]

After that he told me another story of the same sort about a fairy rider, who met a gentleman that was after losing all his fortune but a shilling, and begged the shilling of him. The gentleman gave him the shilling, and the fairy rider – a little red man – rode a horse for him in a race, waving a red handkerchief to him as a signal when he was to double the stakes, and made him a rich man.

Then he gave us an extraordinary English doggerel rhyme which I took down, though it seems singularly incoherent when written out at length. These rhymes are repeated by the old men as a sort of chant, and when a line comes that is more than usually irregular they seem to take a real delight in forcing it into the mould of the recitative. All the time he was chanting the old man kept up a kind of snakelike movement in his body, which seemed to fit the chant and make it part of him.

THE WHITE HORSE

My horse he is white,
Though at first he was bay,
And he took great delight
In travelling by night
    And by day.

His travels were great
If I could but half of them tell,
He was rode in the garden by Adam,
The day that he fell.

On Babylon plains
He ran with speed for the plate,

He was hunted next day
By Hannibal the great.

After that he was hunted
In the chase of a fox,
When Nebuchadnezar ate grass,
In the shape of an ox.

We are told in the next verses of his going into the ark with Noah, of Moses riding him through the Red Sea; then

He was with king Pharaoh in Egypt
When fortune did smile,
And he rode him stately along
The gay banks of the Nile.

He was with king Saul and all
His troubles went through,
He was with king David the day
That Goliath he slew.

For a few verses he is with Juda and Maccabeus the great, with Cyrus, and back again to Babylon. Next we find him as the horse that came into Troy.

When ( ) came to Troy with joy,
My horse he was found,
He crossed over the walls and entered
The city I'm told.

* * *

I come on him again, in Spain,
And he in full bloom,
By Hannibal the great he was rode,
And he crossing the Alps into Rome.

The horse being tall
And the Alps very high,
His rider did fall
And Hannibal the great lost an eye.

Afterwards he carries young Sipho (Scipio), and then he is
ridden by Brian when driving the Danes from Ireland, and by
St Ruth when he fell at the battle of Aughrim, and by Sarsfield
at the siege of Limerick.

> He was with king James who sailed
> To the Irish shore,
> But at last he got lame,
> When the Boyne's bloody battle was o'er.

> He was rode by the greatest of men
> At famed Waterloo,
> Brave Daniel O'Connell he sat
> On his back it is true.

> *   *   *

> Brave Dan's on his back,
> He's ready once more for the field.
> He never will stop till the Tories,
> He'll make them to yield.

Grotesque as this long rhyme appears, it has, as I said, a
sort of existence when it is crooned by the old man at his
fireside, and it has great fame in the island. The old man
himself is hoping that I will print it, for it would not be fair,
he says, that it should die out of the world, and he is the
only man here who knows it, and none of them have ever
heard it on the mainland. He has a couple more examples of
the same kind of doggerel, but I have not taken them
down.[49]

Both in English and in Irish the songs are full of words
the people do not understand themselves, and when they
come to say the words slowly their memory is usually uncertain.

All the morning I have been digging maidenhair ferns with a
boy I met on the rocks, who was in great sorrow because his
father died suddenly a week ago of a pain in his heart.

'We wouldn't have chosen to lose our father for all the gold there is in the world,' he said, 'and it's great loneliness and sorrow there is in the house now.'

Then he told me that a brother of his who is a stoker in the Navy had come home a little while before his father died, and that he had spent all his money in having a fine funeral, with plenty of drink at it, and tobacco.

'My brother has been a long way in the world,' he said, 'and seen great wonders. He does be telling us of the people that do come out to them from Italy, and Spain, and Portugal, and that it is a sort of Irish they do be talking – not English at all – though it is only a word here and there you'd understand.'

When we had dug out enough of roots from the deep crannies in the rocks where they are only to be found, I gave my companion a few pence, and sent him back to his cottage.

The old man who tells me the Irish poems is curiously pleased with the translations I have made from some of them.

He would never be tired, he says, listening while I would be reading them, and they are much finer things than his old bits of rhyme.

Here is one of them, as near the Irish as I am able to make it:

RIOCARD MÓR[50]

I put the sorrow of destruction on the bad luck,
For it would be a pity ever to deny it,
It is to me it is stuck,
My loneliness, my pain, my complaining.

It is the fairy-host
Put me a-wandering
And took from me my goods of the world.

At Mainistir na Ruaidhe
It is on me the shameless deed was done:
Finn Bheara and his fairy-host
Took my little horse on me from under the bag.

If they left me the skin
It would bring me tobacco for three months,
But they did not leave anything with me
But the old minister in its place.

Am not I to be pitied?
My bond and my note are on her,
And the price of her not yet paid,
My loneliness, my pain, my complaining.

The devil a hill or a glen, or highest fort
Ever was built in Ireland,
Is not searched on me for my mare;
And I am still at my complaining.

I got up in the morning,
I put a red spark in my pipe.
I went to the Cnoc Meá
To get satisfaction from them.

I spoke to them,
If it was in them to do a right thing,
To get me my little mare,
Or I would be changing my wits.

'Do you hear, Riocard Mór
It is not here is your mare,
She is in Glenasmoil
With the fairy-men these three months.'

I ran on in my walking,
I followed the road straightly,
I was in Glenasmoil
Before the noon was ended.

I spoke to the fairy-man,
If it was in him to do a right thing,
To get me my little mare,
Or I would be changing my wits.

'Do you hear, Riocard Mór?
It is not here is your mare,
She is in Cnoc Bally Brishlawn
With the horseman of the music these three months.'

I ran off on my walking,
I followed the road straightly,
I was in Cnoc Bally Brishlawn
With the black fall of the night.

That is a place was a crowd
As it was seen by me,
All the weavers of the globe,
It is there you would have news of them.

I spoke to the horseman,
If it was in him to do a right thing,
To get me my little mare,
Or I would be changing my wits.

'Do you hear, Riocard Mór?
It is not here is your mare,
She is in Cnoc Cruachan,
In the back end of the palace.'

I ran off on my walking,
I followed the road straightly,
I made no rest or stop
Till I was in face of the palace.

That is the place was a crowd
As it appeared to me,
The men and women of the country,
And they all making merry.

Arthur Scoil (?) stood up
And began himself giving the lead,
It is joyful, light and active,
I would have danced the course with them.

They drew up on their feet
And they began to laugh,
'Look at Riocard Mór,
And he looking for his little mare.'

I spoke to the man,
And he ugly and humpy,
Unless he would get me my mare
I would break a third of his bones.

'Do you hear, Riocard Mór?
It is not here is your mare,
She is in Alvin of Leinster,
On a halter with my mother.'

I ran off on my walking,
And I came to Alvin of Leinster.
I met the old woman –
On my word she was not pleasing.

I spoke to the old woman,
And she broke out in English:
'Get agone, you rascal,
I don't like your notions.'

'Do you hear, you old woman?
Keep away from me with your English,
But speak to me with the tongue
I hear from every person.'

'It is from me you will get word of her,
Only you come too late –
I made a hunting cap
For Conal Cath of her yesterday.'

I ran off on my walking,
Through roads that were cold and dirty,
I fell in with the fairy-man,
And he lying down on in the Ruaidhe.

'I pity a man without a cow,
I pity a man without a sheep,
But in the case of a man without a horse
It is hard for him to be long in the world.'

This morning, when I had been lying for a long time on a
rock near the sea watching some hooded crows that were dropping shellfish on the rocks to break them, I saw one bird that
had a large white object which it was dropping continually
without any result. I got some stones and tried to drive it off
when the thing had fallen, but several times the bird was too
quick for me and made off with it before I could get down to
him. At last, however, I dropped a stone almost on top of him

and he flew away. I clambered down hastily, and found to my amazement a worn golf-ball! No doubt it had been brought out some way or other from the links in County Clare, which are not far off, and the bird had been trying half the morning to break it.

Further on I had a long talk with a young man who is inquisitive about modern life, and I explained to him an elaborate trick or corner on the Stock Exchange that I heard of lately. When I got him to understand it fully, he shouted with delight and amusement.

'Well,' he said when he was quiet again, 'isn't it a great wonder to think that those rich men are as big rogues as ourselves.'

The old story-teller has given me a long rhyme about a man who fought with an eagle. It is rather irregular and has some obscure passages, but I have translated it with the scholar.

FÉILIM AND THE EAGLE[51]

On my getting up in the morning
And I bothered, on a Sunday,
I put my brogues on me,
And I going to Tierny
In the Glen of the Dead People.
It is there the big eagle fell in with me,
He like a black stack of turf sitting up stately.

I called him a lout and a fool,
The son of a female and a fool,
Of the race of the Clan Cleopas, the biggest rogues in the land.
That and my seven curses
And never a good day to be on you,
Who stole my little cock from me that could crow the sweetest.

'Keep your wits right in you
And don't curse me too greatly,
By my strength and my oath
I never took rent of you,
I didn't grudge what you would have to spare

In the house of the burnt pigeons,
It is always useful you were to men of business.

'But get off home
And ask Nora
What name was on the young woman that scalded his head.
The feathers there were on his ribs
Are burnt on the hearth,
And they eat him and they taking and it wasn't much were thankful.'

'You are a liar, you stealer,
They did not eat him, and they're taking
Nor a taste of the sort without being thankful,
You took him yesterday
As Nora told me,
And the harvest quarter will not be spent till I take a tax of you.'

'Before I lost the Fianna
It was a fine boy I was,
It was not about thieving was my knowledge,
But always putting spells,
Playing games and matches with the strength of Gol Mac Morna,
And you are making me a rogue.
At the end of my life.'

'There is a part of my father's books with me,
Keeping in the bottom of a box,
And when I read them the tears fall down from me.
But I found out in history
That you are a son of the Dearg Mór,
If it is fighting you want and you wont be thankful.'

The Eagle dressed his bravery
With his share of arms and his clothes,
He had the sword that was the sharpest
Could be got anywhere.
I and my scythe with me,
And nothing on but my shirt,
We went at each other early in the day.

We were as two giants
Ploughing in a valley in a glen of the mountains.
We did not know for the while which was the better man.
You could hear the shakes that were on our arms under each other,

From that till the sunset,
Till it was forced on him to give up.

I wrote a 'challenge boxáil' to him
On the morning of the next day,
To come till we would fight without doubt at the dawn of day.
The second fist I drew on him
I struck him on the bone of his jaw,
He fell, and it is no lie there was a cloud in his head.

The Eagle stood up,
He took the end of my hand: —
'You are the finest man I ever saw in my life,
Go off home, my blessing will be on you for ever,
You have saved the fame of Éire for yourself till the Day of the
    Judgement.'

Ah! neighbours, did you hear
The goodness and power of Féilim?
The biggest wild beast you could get,
The second fist he drew on it
He struck it on the jaw,
It fell, and it did not rise
Till the end of two days.

Well as I seem to know these people of the islands, there is
hardly a day that I do not come upon some new, primitive
feature of their life.

Yesterday I went into a cottage where the woman was at
work and very carelessly dressed. She waited for a while till I
got into conversation with her husband, and then she slipped
into the corner and put on a clean petticoat and a bright shawl
round her neck. Then she came back and took her place at the
fire.

This evening I was in another cottage till very late talking to
the people. When the little boy – the only child of the house –
got sleepy, the old grandmother took him on her lap and began
singing to him. As soon as he was drowsy she worked his
clothes off him by degrees, scratching him softly with her nails
as she did so all over his body. Then she washed his feet with a
little water out of a pot and put him into his bed.

When I was going home the wind was driving the sand into my face so that I could hardly find my way. I had to hold my hat over my mouth and nose, and my hand over my eyes while I groped along, with my feet feeling for rocks and holes in the sand.

I have been sitting all the morning with an old man who was making sugawn[52] ropes for his house, and telling me stories while he worked. He was a pilot when he was young, and we had great talk at first about Germans, and Italians, and Russians, and the ways of seaport towns. Then he came round to talk of the middle island, and he told me this story which shows the curious jealousy that is between the islands:

Long ago we used all to be pagans, and the saints used to be coming to teach us about God and the creation of the world. The people on the middle island were the last to keep a hold on the fire-worshipping, or whatever it was they had in those days, but in the long run a saint got in among them and they began listening to him, though they would often say in the evening they believed, and then say the morning after that, they did not believe. In the end the saint gained them over and they began building a church, and the saint had tools that were in use with them for working with the stones. When the church was half-way up the people held a kind of meeting one night among themselves, when the saint was asleep in his bed, to see if they did really believe and no mistake in it.

The leading man got up, and this is what he said: that they should go down and throw their tools over the cliff, for if there was such a man as God, and if the saint was as well known to Him as he said, then he would be as well able to bring up the tools out of the sea as they were to throw them in.

They went then and threw their tools over the cliff.

When the saint came down to the church in the morning the workmen were all sitting on the stones and no work doing.

'For what cause are you idle?' asked the saint.

'We have no tools,' said the men, and then they told him the story of what they had done.

He kneeled down and prayed God that the tools might come up out of the sea, and after that he prayed that no other people might ever be as great fools as the people on the middle island, and that God might preserve their dark minds of folly to them till the end of the world. And that is why no man out of that island can tell you a whole story without stammering, or bring any work to end without a fault in it.[53]

I asked him if he had known old Pat Dirane on the middle island, and heard the fine stories he used to tell.

'No one knew him better than I did,' he said; 'for I do often be in that island making curaghs for the people. One day old Pat came down to me when I was after tarring a new curagh, and he asked me to put a little tar on the knees of his breeches the way the rain wouldn't come through on him.

'I took the brush in my hand, and I had him tarred down to his feet before he knew what I was at. "Turn round the other side now," I said, "and you'll be able to sit where you like." Then he felt the tar coming in hot against his skin and he began cursing my soul, and I was sorry for the trick I'd played on him.'

This old man was the same type as the genial, whimsical old men one meets all through Ireland, and had none of the local characteristics that are so marked on Inishmaan.

When we were tired talking I showed some of my tricks and a little crowd collected. When they were gone another old man who had come up began telling us about the fairies. One night when he was coming home from the lighthouse he heard a man riding on the road behind him, and he stopped to wait for him, but nothing came. Then he heard as if there was a man trying to catch a horse on the rocks, and in a little time he went on. The noise behind him got bigger as he went along as if twenty horses, and then as if a hundred or a thousand, were galloping after him. When he came to the stile where he had to leave the road and got out over it, something hit against him and threw him down on the rock, and a gun he had in his hand fell into the field beyond him.

'I asked the priest we had at that time what was in it,' he said, 'and the priest told me it was the fallen angels; and I don't know but it was.'

'Another time,' he went on, 'I was coming down where there is a bit of a cliff and a little hole under it, and I heard a flute playing in the hole or beside it, and that was before the dawn began. Whatever any one says there are strange things. There was one night thirty years ago a man came down to get my wife to go up to his wife, for she was in childbed.

'He was something to do with the lighthouse or the coast-guards, one of them Protestants who don't believe in any of these things and do be making fun of us. Well, he asked me to go down and get a quart of spirits while my wife would be getting herself ready, and he said he would go down along with me if I was afraid.

'I said I was not afraid, and I went by myself.

'When I was coming back there was something on the path, and wasn't I a foolish fellow, I might have gone to one side or the other over the sand, but I went on straight till I was near it – till I was too near it – then I remembered that I had heard them saying none of those creatures can stand before you and you saying the *De Profundis*, so I began saying it, and the thing ran off over the sand and I got home.

'Some of the people used to say it was only an old jackass that was on the path before me, but I never heard tell of an old jackass would run away from a man and he saying the *De Profundis*.'

I told him the story of the fairy ship which had disappeared when the man made the sign of the cross, as I had heard it on the middle island.

'There do be strange things on the sea,' he said. 'One night I was down there where you can see that green point, and I saw a ship coming in and I wondered what it would be doing coming so close to the rocks. It came straight on towards the place I was in, and then I got frightened and I ran up to the houses, and when the captain saw me running he changed his course and went away.

'Sometimes I used to go out as a pilot at that time – I went a few times only. Well, one Sunday a man came down and said there was a big ship coming into the sound. I ran down with two men and we went out in a curagh; we went round the point where they said the ship was, and there was no ship in it. As it was a Sunday we had nothing to do, and it was a fine calm day, so we rowed out a long way looking for the ship, till I was further than I ever was before or after. When I wanted to turn back we saw a great flock of birds on the water and they all black, without a white bird through them. They had no fear of us at all, and the men with me wanted to go up to them, so we went further. When we were quite close they got up, so many that they blackened the sky, and they lit down again a hundred or maybe a hundred and twenty yards off. We went after them again, and one of the men wanted to kill one with a thole-pin, and the other man wanted to kill one with his rowing stick. I was afraid they would upset the curagh, but they would go after the birds.

'When we were quite close one man threw the pin and the other man hit at them with his rowing stick, and the two of them fell over in the curagh, and she turned on her side and only it was quite calm the lot of us were drowned.

'I think those black gulls and the ship were the same sort, and after that I never went out again as a pilot. It is often curaghs go out to ships and find there is no ship.

'A while ago a curagh went out to a ship from the big island, and there was no ship; and all the men in the curagh were drowned. A fine song was made about them after that, though I never heard it myself.

'Another day a curagh was out fishing from this island, and the men saw a hooker not far from them, and they rowed up to it to get a light for their pipes – at that time there were no matches – and when they up to the big boat it was gone out of its place, and they were in great fear.'

Then he told me a story he had got from the mainland about a man who was driving one night through the country, and met a woman who came up to him and asked him to take her into his cart. He thought something was not right about her, and he went on. When he had gone a little way he looked back, and it was a pig was on the road and not a woman at all.

He thought he was a done man, but he went on. When he was going through a wood further on, two men came out to him, one from each side of the road, and they took hold of the bridle of the horse and led it on between them. They were old stale men with frieze clothes on them, and the old fashions. When they came out of the wood he found people as if there was a fair on the road, with the people buying and selling and they not living people at all. The old men took him through the crowd, and then they left him. When he got home and told the old people of the two old men and the ways and fashions they had about them, the old people told him it was his two grandfathers had taken care of him, for they had a great love for him and he a lad growing up.

This evening we had a dance in the inn parlour, where a fire had been lighted and the tables had been pushed into the corners. There was no master of the ceremonies, and when I had played two or three jigs and other tunes on my fiddle, there was a pause, as I did not know how much of my music the people wanted, or who else could be got to sing or play. For a moment a deadlock seemed to be coming, but a young girl I knew fairly well saw my difficulty, and took the management of our festivities into her hands. At first she asked a coastguard's daughter to play a reel on the mouth organ, which she did at once with admirable spirit and rhythm. Then the little girl asked me to play again, telling me what I should choose, and went on in the same way managing the evening till she thought it was time to go home. Then she stood up, thanked me in Irish, and walked out of the door, without looking at anybody, but followed almost at once by the whole party.

When they had gone I sat for a while on a barrel in the public-house talking to some young men who were reading a paper in Irish. Then I had a long evening with the scholar and two story-tellers – both old men who had been pilots – taking down stories and poems. We were at work for nearly six hours, and the more matter we got the more the old men seemed to remember.

'I was to go out fishing tonight,' said the younger as he came in, 'but I promised you to come, and you're a civil man, so I wouldn't take five pounds to break my word to you. And now' – taking up his glass of whisky – 'here's to your good health, and may you live till they make you a coffin out of a gooseberry bush, or till you die in childbed.'

They drank my health and our work began.

'Have you heard tell of the poet MacSweeny?'[54] said the same man, sitting down near me.

'I have,' I said, 'in the town of Galway.'

'Well,' he said, 'I'll tell you his piece "The Big Wedding", for it's a fine piece and there aren't many that know it. There was a poor servant girl out in the country, and she got married to a poor servant boy. MacSweeny knew the two of them, and he was away at that time and it was a month before he came back. When he came back he went to see Peggy O'Hara – that was the name of the girl – and he asked her if they had had a great wedding. Peggy said it was only middling, but they hadn't forgotten him all the same, and she had a bottle of whisky for him in the cupboard. He sat down by the fire and began drinking the whisky. When he had a couple of glasses taken and was warm by the fire, he began making a song, and this was the song he made about the wedding of Peggy O'Hara.'

He had the poem in both English and Irish, but as it has been found elsewhere and attributed to another folk-poet, I need not give it.

We had another round of porter and whisky, and then the old man who had MacSweeny's wedding gave us a bit of a drinking song,[55] which the scholar took down and I translated with him afterwards:

This is what the old woman says at the Béal-leaca when she sees a man without knowledge –

'Were you ever at the house of the Still, did you ever get a drink from it? Neither wine nor beer is as sweet as it is, but it is well I was not burnt when I fell down after a drink of it by the fire of Mr Sloper.

'I praise Owen O'Hernon over all the doctors of Ireland, it is he put drugs on the water, and it lying on the barley.

'If you gave but a drop of it to an old woman who does be walking the world with a stick, she would think for a week that it was a fine bed was made for her.'

After that I had to get out my fiddle and play some tunes for them while they finished their whisky. A new stock of porter was brought in this morning to the little public-house underneath my room, and I could hear in the intervals of our talk that a number of men had come in to treat some neighbours from the middle island, and were singing many songs, some of them in English of the kind I have given, but most of them in Irish.

A little later when the party broke up downstairs my old men got nervous about the fairies – they live some distance away – and set off across the sandhills.

The next day I left with the steamer.

Notes

INTRODUCTION

1. The Congested Districts Board was set up by Arthur Balfour as
Chief Secretary for Ireland in 1891, to encourage development in
those areas, mainly along the Atlantic seaboard, in which the population was out of proportion with the productive capacity of the land.
(A 'congested district' was initially defined as one in which the total
rateable value per inhabitant was less than thirty shillings.) The main
activities of the CDB were the promotion of local industries and
agriculture, the building of roads and harbours, and the buying-out of
big landlords so that their estates could be subdivided and the former
tenants settled upon holdings of viable extent. (See *Ireland since the
Famine*, F. S. L. Lyons, London, 1971, for the role of the CDB
within the government's policy of 'constructive unionism' in the
1890s; and for a blow-by-blow account of its work, *An Account of the
Congested Districts Board for Ireland from 1891 to 1923* by its former
first secretary, W. L. Micks, London, 1925.)

PART I

2. George Petrie (1790–1866) represents the transformation of
Celtic antiquarianism, with its armchair speculations about the Druids
and the Lost Tribes of Israel, into a recognizably modern archaeology
based on investigation of sites. He was also President of the Royal
Hibernian Academy and published an important collection of Irish
traditional music. He visited Aran and made the first scientific study
of its monuments in 1822, and again in 1857 with the British Association expedition, when he collected many folksongs and painted an
almost expressionistically contorted view of Dún Aonghasa on its
precipice (National Gallery of Ireland). From 1835 to 1842 he directed
the Topographical Department of the Ordnance Survey of Ireland,
for which John O'Donovan travelled the country recording its ancient
monuments, place-names and traditions. (See Dr William Stokes,
Life and Labours in Art and Archaeology of George Petrie, London,
1885.)

Dr William Wilde (1815–76), Dublin's leading eye and ear surgeon, was President of the Royal Irish Academy and catalogued its collections. He also wrote travel books, notably *Lough Corrib and Lough Mask*, on the two great lakes near his country home Moytura House (named from a nearby group of stone circles and other monuments which he identified as the site of the Battle of Moytura, now regarded as mythical, between the Fir Bolg and the Tuatha Dé Danann). He conducted the British Association's visit to Aran in 1857, and was knighted in 1864 for his services to the Irish census. His wife Lady Wilde wrote patriotic poems and books on folklore, and their son was the famous and infamous Oscar.

The eminent Danish linguist Holger Pedersen (1867–1953), professor at Copenhagen, was noted for the scope of his researches into Indo-European, Semitic and Finno-Ugaric languages. His doctorate, 'Aspiration in Irish', dates from 1897 and his *Comparative Grammar of the Celtic Languages* was published in 1903–13. His disciple Franz Nikolaus Finck spent four months in Aran in 1894/5 researching his thesis, which was published as part of his two-volume *Die araner Mundart* (Marburg, 1899). An Aran-born writer, the late Breandán Ó hEithir, has disinterred from this work the phrase 'Ní bhéarfainn broim dreóilín ar dhuilleog cuilinn agus is beag an puth gaoth é sin!' ('I wouldn't give the fart of a wren on a hollyleaf, and it's the small puff of wind that is!'), which the linguistic anarchs of Synge's plays would be hard pressed to emulate.

The American linguist and antiquarian Jeremia Curtin (?1840–1906) was reputed to know seventy languages. As Secretary of the US Legation in St Petersburg he studied and translated from Slavonic languages. In 1883–91 with the Bureau of Ethnology of the Smithsonian Institute he worked on North American Indian languages. His *Myths and Folklore of Ireland* appeared in 1890.

3. Dun (pronounced 'doon', from the Irish *dún*), a large stone ringfort or cashel. (See note 16, below.)

4. Synge's uncle, the Rev. Alexander Hamilton Synge (1820–72), was the Protestant minister of the Aran Islands in the years 1851–5. His letters make it clear that he hated the isolation and discomfort of the islands, and despised their 'papist' inhabitants. ('Here I am Lord of all I survey – surrounded by dirt and ignorance.') His congregation consisted of about twenty-five coastguards and policemen, and, although he established Protestant schools in Cill Mhuirbhigh in the west of Árainn and in Inis Oírr, on the whole he seems not to have pressed his dogmas on the islanders, and to have devoted most of his

energy to fishing with his smack, the *Georgiana*. At that time the fishermen of the Claddagh, a 'native' settlement on the outskirts of Galway, claimed the fishing rights of Galway Bay, and there were several arguments between them and the Rev. Synge and his Aran crew. On one occasion the minister was hit by a stone, and held off a boarding party only by threatening them with his gun. After another such attack on his and other boats a gunboat was dispatched to keep the peace in the bay, and the Rev. Synge, accompanied by police, went into the Claddagh to identify the culprits, who appeared in court as a result and were bound over on a promise of good behaviour. (See Paul F. Botheroyd, 'The Rev. Alexander Hamilton Synge in the Aran Islands', *Cahiers Irlandais*, Rennes, 1983.)

5. Beehive dwellings, or, as Synge calls them elsewhere, cloghauns (from the Irish *clochán*), are dry-stone huts, usually rectangular or oval at foundation level, and roofed by corbelling the walls inwards (i.e., with each course of stones slightly overhanging the previous one) until the top could be finished off with a row of flat slabs. The one Synge mentions here is called Clochán na Carraige (from An Charraig, the rock, the name of the area in which it is located), and is one of the best preserved in the country. It is 19 feet long and over 8 feet high inside, and has two 3-foot high doors opposite each other as in the traditional cottage, and a tiny window in one end. Like most other such huts on the islands it probably dates from early Christian times.

6. Teampall an Cheathrair Álainn, the 'church of the four beautiful persons', is a small fifteenth-century Gothic chapel, roofless but otherwise well preserved, and beautifully situated among little stone-walled pastures. The Ceathrar Álainn are traditionally identified as the saints Fursey, Brendan of Birr, Conall and Berchan. The story Synge was told of the nearby holy well suggested to him part of the plot of his play *The Well of the Saints*. In the version of the story most current on the island today, a blind lad is brought to the vicinity by his mother but finds the well by himself, and is instantly cured.

7. Poteen (from the Irish *poitín*), illicitly distilled barley spirits. The remains of a few little stillhouses can be found in Inis Meáin, and one or two in Árainn, but nowadays most *poitín* comes in from Connemara, where it is made in large quantities despite repeated police raids.

8. The story of Diarmaid and Gráinne is one of the best known of Irish myths. Gráinne, engaged to Fionn Mac Cumhal, the elderly chief of the warrior band known as the Fianna, persuades Diarmaid, handsomest of his men, to run away with her. Pursued by Fionn, they

move from place to place around Ireland, but eventually obtain Fionn's forgiveness. Country folk used to imagine that the late Stone Age tombs made of huge slabs of rock found in most parts of Ireland were the beds Diarmaid and Gráinne built for themselves. In Árainn there are two such tombs now visible, the one mentioned by Synge in the east of the island being lost beneath shifting sand, and in his time there were at least three to be seen in Inis Meáin, but he makes no mention of them. At least one man from Fearann an Choirce in Árainn remembers hearing that Diarmaid was burned to death at the 'bed of Diarmaid and Gráinne' just north of that village; this appears to be a local variant of the legend.

9. The *curach* (usually anglicized as 'currach'), a canoe for two to four rowers, made of tarred canvas stretched over a framework of laths and timbers, is still in use in Aran and elsewhere on the Atlantic coast of Ireland. Being keelless and light, it can be run ashore on a pebbly beach or on shelving rocks and quickly carried up out of reach of the waves. Medieval legends tell of monks making long sea voyages in large sailing currachs of hide, and they may in fact have reached Iceland in this way (E. Estyn Evans, *Irish Folk Ways*, London, 1957).

10. The hulk full of Norwegian ice was provided by the Congested Districts Board so that fish landed in Aran could be iced before transport to Galway.

11. These moccasin-like shoes, which long ago were made of seal-skin, are still worn by a few men in Inis Meáin. They have always been known in Aran as *bróga úrleathair*, 'rawhide shoes'. The strange word 'pampootie' was (according to local lore recorded in the *Folklore Journal*, 2, 1884) introduced by an East Indian ship's captain who settled in Inis Oírr some two hundred or more years earlier, and it has probably always been more popular with visitors than with the islanders themselves. It has been tentatively derived from various words for 'slipper' in Dutch, Spanish, Turkish and even Javanese.

12. Note that Synge does not mention the famous 'traditional' Aran sweater with its variety of patterns allegedly peculiar to particular families and handed down from time immemorial. In fact Aran knitting was the creation of the CDB, and most of its stitches are found in other parts of the Atlantic seaboard (as the term 'ganzy', i.e., Guernsey, reminds one); some of these stitches are said to have been brought in by Scottish women employed in curing fish, while others were learned from patterns sent home by emigrants in America. The often repeated lore that these stitches are used in the identification of drowned men is a fabrication, and owes something to *Riders to the*

Sea, in which a body is identified by the number of dropped stitches in a plain stocking.

13. Antti Aarne and Stith Thompson's *The Types of the Folktale* (Helsinki, 1973) lists many variants of the tale, 'A Pound of Flesh', which has been recorded widely from Scandinavia to Turkey; Shakespeare's *Merchant of Venice* is of course the most famous literary treatment of the theme. Here it is combined with the tale of 'The Wager on the Wife's Chastity', which, like the other, is known from all over Ireland. Synge published the present version as 'A Story from Inishmaan' in the *New Ireland Review* of November 1898.

14. The hooker was the traditional wooden workboat of the Galway Bay area, used for fishing and transport. The elegance and daring of its lines have puzzled marine historians, but it seems to have evolved locally. Its massive-timbered tar-black hull, up to 44 feet long, has high round bows to face the Atlantic waves, a short foredeck and a square stern; it carries a single mast and a bowsprit, and its three canvas sails are almost invariably of a rich brown colour. When lorries became the usual means of transport between Galway and the coastal villages of Connemara, the hookers were left to rot in muddy creeks, but some of them – including one or two famous ones that Synge would have seen – have been preserved and are sailed at various regattas around the bay. (See Richard Scott, *The Galway Hookers*, Dublin, 1983.)

15. The Aran Islands have no indigenous fuel supplies apart from the dried cow-dung mentioned elsewhere by Synge, and which is still occasionally used. Many families of the equally poverty-stricken south Connemara coast lived by cutting and drying turf from the peat bogs and shipping it to the Aran Islands – a trade that finally died only in the 1960s, as coal and bottled propane gas became more easily available.

16. Dún Chonchúir (usually anglicized as Doonconnor) is the most impressive cashel of the islands after Dún Aonghasa in Árainn. Its main wall forms an oval 227 feet long by 115 feet broad, and consists of three independently constructed layers totalling 19 feet in thickness; each is raised to a different height to make two terrace-like steps around the interior of the wall, the outermost layer being 20 feet high in places. A slighter outer wall links this central enclosure to a terraced rectangular bastion to the east, and on the west it overhangs a steep glen. In the mythical history of the invasions of Ireland, Conchúr was the brother of Aonghas, who is credited with the building of Dún Aonghasa.

17. The Fir Bolg were a people who figure in the corpus of Celtic myth that was by degrees Christianized, rationalized and compiled into a credible history of Ireland by monastic scribes in the eighth to the fifteenth centuries. According to the medieval text called *Lebor Gabála Érenn* ('The Book of the Taking of Ireland'), the Fir Bolg were the fourth of the groups who successively conquered and settled Ireland; they were expelled by the Tuatha Dé Danann (the people of the goddess Dana) but later returned and settled in Aran under their leader Aonghas, before their final defeat by the last wave of invaders, the Goidel. In Synge's day most scholars believed there was some truth in this account, and indeed the belief is still not extinct; the Fir Bolg used to be identified with the Belgae, a Celtic tribe with whom Julius Caesar had dealings.

18. This folktale, 'The Loving Wife', has been recorded from various European countries, Russia, Spanish America, India and Africa (Antti Aarne and Stith Thompson, *The Types of the Folktale*, Helsinki, 1973). It provided Synge with the basic situation of his *The Shadow of the Glen*, written in 1902 and first performed the following year.

19. The keen (Irish *caoineadh*, 'lament') died out early in this century, as islanders came to feel it was particularly associated with their 'backwardness', but it has been recorded from an Aran woman who died only a few years ago. In his notebook entry on this burial Synge mentions that the priest had held a service over the dead woman the previous day, and had then been recalled to Árainn. The story he is told of the two men falling down drunk in the graveyard supplied him with a grotesquerie for *The Playboy of the Western World*.

20. The burning of seaweed for its ash, as a source of alkalies for the growing industries of glass-making, linen-bleaching, etc., started, it seems, in the West of Ireland in about 1700 and spread soon after to the Atlantic coast of Scotland, as supplies of wood ash decreased. Alternative supplies of soda and potash became available in the early nineteenth century, but the discovery of iodine and its antiseptic properties gave the kelp industry a further century of life, and it died out only with the introduction of penicillin. In Aran the last kelp was made in about 1948.

21. Miss Digby of Landenstown, Kildare, had died by 1894, and the property had passed to two sisters, Geraldine Digby St Lawrence and Lady Henrietta Eliza Guinness. (See note in the introductory essay, p. xiii.)

22. This tale is of the universally distributed type known as 'The

Dragon-Slayer' (Antti Aarne and Stith Thompson, *The Types of the Folktale*, Helsinki, 1973), with introductory elements from other widely known types. An elaborate version of it collected in the west of Connemara is given in the Irish in *Siamsa an Gheimhridh* by Dónall O'Fotharta (Dublin, 1892).

23. The change in ownership of the islands with the death of Miss Digby brought the bailiff down on the people, just at a period of extreme want due to successive failures of the potato crop and a fall in kelp and pig prices, coinciding with outbreaks of flu from which many died. Many tenants had arrears of six to nine years' rent; the landlords were prepared to settle for two years, but refused the priest's plea to remit all arrears because of the near famine conditions. In 1884 the bailiff with an escort of constables evicted twelve households in the big island, ten of these being readmitted to their homes (no doubt on a caretakers' agreement that left them no security of tenure). In Inis Meáin one household was evicted and three came to an agreement with the landlords' agent. In 1886 the bailiff returned with fifteen policemen and evicted a dozen households from the western village of Eoghanacht in the big island (some of them owed nineteen years' rent, and even the agent had admitted they were too poor to pay anything), but on that occasion storms prevented the bailiff coming to Inis Meáin. A fine of £452 had been imposed on the tenantry of the islands for damages caused during the Land War of 1880/81, and many were still refusing to pay this despite the urgings of the parish priest Fr Farragher and his bishop. In January 1898 an attempt to collect this money with the help of fifteen constables was beaten off by a crowd of three hundred tenants in the big island. In May a rent-collecting invasion of Inis Meáin was once again thwarted by a sudden storm, but on the 11th of June the forces of justice returned, with the results Synge witnessed. These seem to have been the last evictions in the islands, although with the growth of the United Irish League from 1908 there was a general determination not to pay rents until the owners agreed to sell out. (See Antoine Powell [an island author], *Oileáin Árann, stair na n-oileán anuas go dtí 1922*, Dublin [n.d. but *c*. 1983].)

24. 'The Magic Bird-heart' tale has been recorded throughout Europe, and in Buddhist mythology (Antti Aarne and Stith Thompson, *The Types of the Folktale*, Helsinki, 1973).

25. These shortcomings of the piers and slips are still a source of anger among the islanders. In the two smaller islands, as of 1991, goods still have to be taken by currach to and from the ferry while it

drifts offshore, and in rough weather this is a long ordeal; it is hoped that the more modern boat that is now being introduced will obviate this obstacle to development.

26. Here is the germ of *The Playboy of the Western World*. (See also the footnote to the introductory essay, p. xxxiv.)

27. The magistrate referred to was the principal middleman of the big island, Patrick O'Flaherty JP (1782–1864) of what was later known as Kilmurvey House; he used to summon defendants to appear before him in his cattleyard 'on the first fine day' and would hand those condemned to prison a committal warrant, whereupon they would take themselves off to Galway at their own expense. (Synge would have read about this procedure in Emily Lawless's *Grania*, published in 1892, and her source would have been Oliver J. Burke's *The South Isles of Aran*, London, 1887.)

28. An old mnemonic for the principal pattern days (i.e. festivals of the patron saints) of the area was:

> Lá 'l Chaomháin in Inis Oírr
> Lá tSin Sheáin in Inis Meáin
> Lá Pheadair is Phóil in Árainn Mhór
> Lá Mhic Dara i gConamara.

(St Cavan's Day in Inis Oírr, St John's Day in Inis Meáin, Sts Peter and Paul's Day in Árainn Mhór, St Macdara's Day in Connemara.) These festivals are still marked by sporting contests and music, as well as by religious ceremonies and visits to the holy places of the islands.

29. The custom of lighting bonfires on St John's Eve still persists; in Aran each village has its bonfire site, and the fires of Connemara are visible across the bay. These midsummer fires had magical significances. Cattle used to be driven through the embers, or between two fires, to ensure their well-being, and glowing sticks or turf sods would be carried to each house or flung into the fields of crops.

30. The Gaelic League, or Conradh na Gaeilge, was founded in Dublin in 1893 by 'a half dozen nonentities', as Douglas Hyde, their first president, put it. Its policy was to foster an 'Irish-speaking Ireland', and the inspirational dedication of these early cultural revolutionaries can be judged by the contrast between the late nineteenth century, when Irish-speaking parents in collaboration with National School teachers were actively beating Irish out of their children, and the early decades of the twentieth century, when up to 75,000 people

were trying to learn the language and participating in Irish dancing and folklore classes, festivals celebrating Irish culture, and Irish games. The League was progressively politicized by such members as Patrick Pearse, and Hyde retired in 1915 when it declared, against his wishes, that it stood for a free Ireland. He was replaced the next year by Eoin MacNeill, then in prison for his part in the 1916 Easter Rising. (Pearse, b. 1879, was executed as a leader of this Rising; for Hyde, see note 33 below.) In 1923, writing for the *Manchester Guardian*, Hyde summarized the influence of the League as follows:

> The Gaelic League grew up and became the spiritual father of Sinn Féin, and Sinn Féin's progeny were the Volunteers, who forced the English to make the Treaty. The Dáil [the Irish parliament] is the child of the Volunteers, and thus it descends directly from the Gaelic League.

The young Patrick Pearse visited Inis Meáin in 1898 and met there an islander home on a visit from Mexico, Tomás Bán Ó Concheanainn (his brother had established the well-known Concannon vineyards in California, which supplied Ireland with communion wine). Tomás had visited branches of the Gaelic League in many American cities and was to become the League's most redoubtable *timire taistil*, or roving organizer. At his suggestion and in consultation with the parish priest, Fr Farragher, a branch of the League was inaugurated in Cill Rónáin in August; the attendance of seven hundred people included a large delegation from Inis Meáin headed by its National School teacher. (See *The Gaelic League Idea*, ed. Seán Ó Tuama, Dublin, 1972, and for the setting up of the Aran branch, the League's organ *Fáinne an Lae*, 20 August 1898.)

31. *Mise do chara go buan*, 'I am your constant friend', a conventional letter-ending equivalent to 'Yours sincerely'.

PART II

32. 'Dear noble Person' is a literal translation of the conventional form of address used in letters, *A dhuine uasal*, the equivalent of 'Dear sir'.

33. *The Love Songs of Connaught* by Douglas Hyde (Dublin, 1893), an influential and pioneering collection of folksongs in Irish. Hyde (1860–1949) made the restoration of Irish culture his life's work. As well as founding the Gaelic League (see note 30), he wrote the first

modern play in Irish (*Casadh an tSúgáin*, 1901) and the collection of folktales mentioned by Synge on p. 85, *Beside the Fire* (1890), and was Professor of Modern Irish in the National University. He became President of the Irish Republic in 1938.

34. A local women's branch, or *Craobh na mBan*, of the Gaelic League was formed in Inis Meáin soon after the foundation of the League branch itself, which was chiefly for the men. Úna Ní Fhaircheallaigh (Agnes O'Farrelly, later Professor of Irish in University College, Dublin) was staying in the MacDonncha cottage at the time to learn Irish, and describes the event in her booklet *Smuainte ar Árainn* (Dublin, 1902).

35. The Stations is the annual custom – still practised by the priests of many rural western parishes – of hearing confessions and celebrating the Mass in a parishioner's house, the honour passing from house to house in rotation within each community. In Synge's day in Inis Meáin there were two Stations each year, one in each of the two 'townlands' into which the island is divided. Since about 1981 there have been four Stations each year, one in each of the four principal villages. (Information from An tAthair Pádraig Standún, the curate in Inis Meáin.)

36. Charles Stewart Parnell (1846–91), a Protestant landowner from Avondale in Co. Wicklow, became the most charismatic figure of the Home Rule movement. He was the first President of the Land League from 1879 and leader of the Irish Parliamentary Party at Westminster from 1880. He was deserted by most of his supporters after being cited as co-respondent in the Katharine O'Shea divorce case in 1889. The occasion Synge is referring to was the eighth anniversary of his death, which, following so soon after his 'betrayal', had left the Home Rule movement plunged into grief, guilt and confusion.

PART III

37. The *feis*, or Irish language festival, was an open-air event, with storytelling, dancing and games, organized by Tomás Ó Concheanainn and chaired by Fr Michael O'Hickey (who was Vice-President of the Gaelic League until 1903, and Professor of Irish at Maynooth, the seminary in which he formed a generation of nationalistic priests).

38. *Mise le mór mheas ort a chara*, I am, with great respect to you, my friend', a conventional letter-ending.

39. The incident is the basis of Synge's play *Riders to the Sea*, written in 1902 and first performed in 1904.

40. On the evening of the 28th of December, 1899, a number of fishermen were sleeping in their boats at anchor in the bay of Cill Éinne, in readiness for an early start the next morning, when a storm struck from the north. Three boats were smashed on the shore, and four men drowned. It was a dreadful blow for Aran's new fishing fleet, so recently established by the CDB. (See Antoine Powell, *Oileáin Árann, stair na n-oileán anuas go dtí 1922*, Dublin [n.d. but *c.* 1983].)

41. The cess (probably from the obsolete noun 'assess') was the rates.

42. The spa is Lisdoonvarna, where the farmers of Co. Clare and neighbouring regions congregate after the harvest, and where matchmakers still operate. Tea-dances there are favoured meeting-places for shy country people seeking mates.

43. A shebeener is a frequenter of the *síbín*, or illicit drinking house.

44. The relative was Synge's uncle, the Rev. Alexander Hamilton Synge. (See note 4 above.)

45. John MacHale (1791–1881), Professor at Maynooth, later Archbishop of Tuam (when he was known as the Lion of the West). A passionate nationalist and supporter of the Irish language, he refused to allow the setting up of National Schools in his diocese (which included Aran) because their teaching was through the medium of English. Island tradition has it that he visited Inis Meáin in 1840 to bless the new chapel, and in 1877. His numerous works in Connacht Irish include translations of Moore's *Irish Melodies*. Thomas Moore (1779–1852), a popular, nationalistic and sentimental Irish poet, was a friend and biographer of Byron.

PART IV

46. Versions of this fairy legend, 'An Bhean a Tógadh As' ('The Woman Who Was Carried Off') have been collected all over Ireland. There are several similar stories in the collection of folklore made by the schoolchildren of the island in 1930 and recently published as *Seanchas Inis Meáin* (ed. Ciarán Ó Coigligh, Dublin, 1990). *Oíche Shamhna*, or Hallowe'en, is the eve of the first of November, one of the two great festivals of the Celtic year; *Oíche Bhealtaine* is the eve of the other, May Day. It used to be believed in Ireland that the fairies changed their seasonal quarters at these times. The idea that

the fairies move from one side of the island to the other on these two evenings is not quite dead in Árainn.

47. A small structure in which Synge often used to sit, a low, three-quarter-circle wall of massive stones on the brink of the highest cliff of Inis Meáin, still called Cathaoir Synge, 'Synge's Chair'. It is obviously ancient but its original purpose is not clear, though probably it was some sort of look-out post.

48. Charlie Lambert was an eighteenth-century squire of Creg Clare in Co. Galway. Stories of the man who is so good at some sport he is forbidden to take part in it were popular in Irish sporting lore, and the theme of 'apparent bilocation' probably originated in a tradition about a seventeenth-century English highwayman who robbed someone near London, rode north and established an alibi by appearing in York on the same day (Dáithí Ó hÓgáin, *The Hero in Irish Folk History*, Dublin and New York, 1985).

49. Such humorous songs exhibiting biblical, classical or historical knowledge were a popular genre in the eighteenth and nineteenth centuries. Synge recorded another seventeen stanzas of this one in the same vein which he did not print; they can be found in *J. M. Synge: Collected Works*, Vol. II, Prose (ed. Alan Price, Oxford, 1966).

50. 'Riocard Mór', 'Big Richard'. Some verses of this folksong recorded in Connemara in the 1930s were attributed to a Seán Bacach Ó Guairim (see Ríonach Ní Fhlathartaigh, *Clár Amhrán Bhaile na hInse*, Dublin, 1976), and a version of it called 'Láirín Riocaird Mhóir' ('Big Richard's Little Mare') was collected in Galway, also in the 1930s. A scrap of lore in Irish from Carna in Connemara and dated 1933 reads 'Riocard Mór. This was a man who lived about seventy years ago and he had a fine horse and it died although it was very healthy one evening. When he saw her in the morning she was gone and an old, useless horse was there instead. It was probably the good people who took her away.' (Information from Dr Ríonach Ní Ógáin, Department of Irish Folklore, University College Dublin.) 'The good people' is a euphemism for the fairies. Cnoc Meá is an isolated hill in east Galway, regarded as the principal fairy stronghold of the region. Cruachan is a group of prehistoric earthworks in Roscommon said to have been the inauguration place of the kings of Connacht. Glenasmoil could be the Gleann na Smól ('Glen of the Thrushes') near Dublin. Other place-names mentioned in the song have not been identified.

51. 'Féilim and the Eagle': this is 'An tIolrach Mór' ('The Big Eagle') by a folk-poet of south Connemara, Féilim Mac Dhubhghaill, who kept a small cornmill in the island of Garomna in the 1830s.

More of the fun of the song is apparent if one knows the circumstances of its production. A woman called on Féilim's wife Nora one day when he was away, and the two women killed a big cock for their dinner, and singed the feathers off it. When Féilim returned and asked what had become of the cock, his wife told him the big eagle had carried it off. But Féilim already knew the truth, and he made up this song scolding the eagle in place of his wife. In the first verse Tierny is Tír an Fhia in Garomna, and the Glen of the Dead People is Gleann an Fhir Mhairbh in An Cheathrú Rua near by. The song has been published in *Amhráin Chlainne Gaedheal* (eds. M. and T. Ó Máille, Dublin, 1905), and some lore about the poet can be found in Peadar Ó Direáin, *Sgéalta na nOileán*, (Dublin, 1929).

52. *súgán*, 'straw rope'.

53. This is a fairly well-known tale of a type called *scéalta bunúis* (aetiological tales, which explain the origin of some state of affairs). Usually the tools are seen by the disbelievers to float on the water, thus confirming the saint's goodness and faith. This story is still remembered in Inis Meáin and Inis Oírr.

54. Mícheál Mac Suibhne (*c.* 1760–*c.* 1820), the best known of Connemara's folk poets, who lived most of his life in the Clifden area. (See Tomás Ó Máille, *Mícheál Mhac Suibhne agus Filidh an t.Sléibhe*, Dublin, 1934.) 'Banais Pheigí ní Eaghra' ('Peggy O'Hara's Wedding'), a comic song full of local references, has often been reprinted since it was first published as an appendix to James Hardiman's edition of Roderic O'Flaherty's *West or H-Iar Connaught* (Dublin, 1846).

55. The drinking song unattributed by Synge is also the work of Mac Suibhne, and is to be found in Douglas Hyde's *The Songs of Connaught* (first published serially in the *Nation* in 1890, republished in book form, Dublin, 1985). It is called 'Fuisce Mháistir Sloper', 'Mr Sloper's Whiskey'. The place-name Synge noted as Beul-leaca does not occur in Hyde's or Ó Máille's versions of the song, and it allows the identification of Mr Sloper with a man of that name who lived at what is still called Sloper's Cliff in Belleek or Béal Leice near Clifden in the time of Mac Suibhne.

READ MORE IN PENGUIN

In every corner of the world, on every subject under the sun, Penguin represents quality and variety – the very best in publishing today.

For complete information about books available from Penguin – including Puffins, Penguin Classics and Arkana – and how to order them, write to us at the appropriate address below. Please note that for copyright reasons the selection of books varies from country to country.

In the United Kingdom: Please write to *Dept. EP, Penguin Books Ltd, Bath Road, Harmondsworth, West Drayton, Middlesex UB7 0DA*

In the United States: Please write to *Consumer Sales, Penguin Putnam Inc., P.O. Box 12289 Dept. B, Newark, New Jersey 07101-5289.* VISA and MasterCard holders call 1-800-788-6262 to order Penguin titles

In Canada: Please write to *Penguin Books Canada Ltd, 10 Alcorn Avenue, Suite 300, Toronto, Ontario M4V 3B2*

In Australia: Please write to *Penguin Books Australia Ltd, P.O. Box 257, Ringwood, Victoria 3134*

In New Zealand: Please write to *Penguin Books (NZ) Ltd, Private Bag 102902, North Shore Mail Centre, Auckland 10*

In India: Please write to *Penguin Books India Pvt Ltd, 11 Community Centre, Panchsheel Park, New Delhi 110017*

In the Netherlands: Please write to *Penguin Books Netherlands bv, Postbus 3507, NL-1001 AH Amsterdam*

In Germany: Please write to *Penguin Books Deutschland GmbH, Metzlerstrasse 26, 60594 Frankfurt am Main*

In Spain: Please write to *Penguin Books S. A., Bravo Murillo 19, 1° B, 28015 Madrid*

In Italy: Please write to *Penguin Italia s.r.l., Via Benedetto Croce 2, 20094 Corsico, Milano*

In France: Please write to *Penguin France, Le Carré Wilson, 62 rue Benjamin Baillaud, 31500 Toulouse*

In Japan: Please write to *Penguin Books Japan Ltd, Kaneko Building, 2-3-25 Koraku, Bunkyo-Ku, Tokyo 112*

In South Africa: Please write to *Penguin Books South Africa (Pty) Ltd, Private Bag X14, Parkview, 2122 Johannesburg*

READ MORE IN PENGUIN

A CHOICE OF TWENTIETH-CENTURY CLASSICS

Ulysses   James Joyce

Ulysses is unquestionably one of the supreme masterpieces, in any artistic form, of the twentieth century. 'It is the book to which we are all indebted and from which none of us can escape' T. S. Eliot

The First Man   Albert Camus

'It is the most brilliant semi-autobiographical account of an Algerian childhood amongst the grinding poverty and stoicism of poor French-Algerian colonials' J. G. Ballard. 'A kind of magical Rosetta stone to his entire career, illuminating both his life and his work with stunning candour and passion' *The New York Times*

Flying Home   Ralph Ellison

Drawing on his early experience – his father's death when he was three, hoboeing his way on a freight train to follow his dream of becoming a musician – Ellison creates stories which, according to the *Washington Post*, 'approach the simple elegance of Chekhov.' 'A shining instalment' *The New York Times Book Review*

Cider with Rosie   Laurie Lee

'Laurie Lee's account of childhood and youth in the Cotswolds remains as fresh and full of joy and gratitude for youth and its sensations as when it first appeared. It sings in the memory' *Sunday Times*. 'A work of art' Harold Nicolson

Kangaroo   D. H. Lawrence

Escaping from the decay and torment of post-war Europe, Richard and Harriett Somers arrive in Australia to a new and freer life. Somers, a disillusioned writer, becomes involved with an extreme political group. At its head is the enigmatic Kangaroo.

READ MORE IN PENGUIN

also published:

by J. M. Synge, W. B. Yeats, and Sean O'Casey

The Playboy of the Western World and Two Other Irish Plays

Riots greeted the first performance of *The Playboy of the Western World* at Dublin's Abbey Theatre on 26 January 1907. Eggs, potatoes and even a slice of fruit cake were hurled at the actors during subsequent performances, and it seems unlikely that much of the actual play could have been heard in the uproar.

Synge's *The Playboy of the Western World*, with the other two plays in this volume, Yeats's *The Countess Cathleen* (1892) and O'Casey's *Cock-a-Doodle Dandy* (1949), mark vital stages in the rich explosion of Irish drama that first made itself heard at the turn of the century and gathered momentum during the Easter Rising of 1916 and the Civil War.